The Student Edition of
SIMULINK®

Dynamic System Simulation Software
for Technical Education

User's Guide

The MATLAB® Curriculum Series

 PRENTICE HALL, Englewood Cliffs, NJ 07632

The MATH WORKS Inc.

Acquisitions Editor: Tom Robbins
Production Editor: Joe Scordato
Cover Designer: The MathWorks, Inc.
Buyer: Donna Sullivan
Editorial Assistant: Phyllis Morgan

Printed in the United States of America

10 9 8 7 6 5 4 3 2 1

ISBN 0-13-452435-7

Prentice-Hall International (UK) Limited, London
Prentice-Hall of Australia Pty. Limited, Sydney
Prentice-Hall Canada Inc., Toronto
Prentice-Hall Hispanoamericana, S.A., Mexico
Prentice-Hall of India Private Limited, New Delhi
Prentice-Hall of Japan, Inc., Tokyo
Simon & Schuster Asia Pte. Ltd., Singapore
Editora Prentice-Hall do Brasil, Ltda., Rio de Janeiro

Contents

Preface

To the Instructor

SIMULINK® is a package for use with MATLAB® for modeling, simulating, and analyzing dynamical systems. Its graphical modeling environment uses familiar block diagrams, so systems illustrated in texts can be easily implemented in SIMULINK. The simulation is interactive, so you can change parameters and immediately see what happens. The analysis tools include those built into SIMULINK, plus the many tools in MATLAB and its application toolboxes. This combination of ease of use with flexible and powerful capability has already made SIMULINK the choice for thousands of engineers, instructors, and students in industry and academia.

Now, The Student Edition of SIMULINK, in combination with The Student Edition of MATLAB, gives students an affordable way to use this powerful modeling and simulation environment in their studies, while learning a tool that will prove invaluable throughout their careers.

SIMULINK allows students to move beyond idealized linear models, to explore more realistic nonlinear models that account for friction, air resistance, gear slippage, and other real-world phenomena. It turns the student's computer into a virtual laboratory for doing detailed analysis and understanding of systems that simply wouldn't be possible or practical otherwise. These systems might describe the response of an electric motor, the flight dynamics of an airplane, the active suspension system of a car, or the effect of the monetary supply on the economy. And it makes it fun.

The Student Edition of SIMULINK for the student's own personal computer is an excellent complement to educationally discounted licenses of the professional version, such as computer lab licenses or workstation site licenses. SIMULINK models are fully compatible, both between the student and professional versions and across computer platforms. As a result, students can take their models to the lab to use advanced tools like the code generation or real-time hardware support provided by the SIMULINK Real-Time Workshop.

By itself, or when coupled with texts, SIMULINK can be effectively incorporated into the curriculum to enhance students' modeling and analysis skills, plus understanding of system dynamics and behavior.

Technical Support for Instructors

The MathWorks provides technical support to registered instructors who use The Student Edition of SIMULINK in their courses.

For technical support questions, instructors can direct inquiries

- Via e-mail: support@mathworks.com
- Via telephone: (508) 653-1415 ext. 4300
- Via fax: (508) 653-2997

Other Information Sources for Instructors and Students

- Use the SIMULINK online help facility by typing help simulink at the MATLAB prompt.

- Students and instructors with access to Usenet newsgroups can participate in the comp.soft-sys.matlab newsgroup. Here, an active community of MATLAB and SIMULINK users – spanning industries, countries, applications, and schools – exchange ideas, help with each other's questions and problems, and share user-written functions and tools. Members of The Math-Works staff also participate, and the newsgroup has become a stimulating, open, and free-flowing forum.

- On the World Wide Web (WWW), use Mosaic or another browser to reach The MathWorks Home Page using the URL http://www.mathworks.com.

- The MathWorks maintains an electronic archive of user-contributed routines, product information, and other useful things. It can be reached using anonymous ftp to ftp.mathworks.com, or from the MATLAB Forum in the MathWorks Home Page on the WWW.

- The quarterly MathWorks newsletter *MATLAB News & Notes* provides information on new products, technical notes and tips, application articles, a calendar of trade shows and conferences, and other useful information. *MATLAB News & Notes* is free to registered users of The Student Edition of SIMULINK.

MATLAB-Based Books

A number of books can be used with the student editions of MATLAB and SIMULINK, many featuring exercises, problem sets, and supplemental functions. These include standard texts or supplemental workbooks in a broad range of courses, such as Control Theory, Signals and Systems, and Linear Systems.

For a current list of MATLAB-based books, consult the MathWorks Home Page on the WWW at http://www.mathworks.com in the MATLAB Forum or the MathWorks anonymous ftp server at ftp.mathworks.com in pub/books/booklist. Or contact your MathWorks educational account representative at (508) 653-1415 (e-mail: info@mathworks.com).

Acknowledgments

The Student Edition of SIMULINK is the product of a collaborative effort between The MathWorks and Prentice Hall, with many people contributing to its development. At The MathWorks, we especially want to acknowledge Rick Spada, Michael Cooperman, Andy Grace, Gary Levenson, Scott French, Luis Bascones, Anna Fiehler, Paul Carter, Donna Sullivan, Liz Callanan, Roy Lurie, and Jim Tung. At Prentice Hall, there have been contributions from Marcia Horton, Tom Robbins, Phyllis Morgan, Joe Scordato, Gary June, Amy Rosen, Paula Maylahn, Joe Sengotta, Donna Sullivan, Frank Nicolazzo, and Don Fowley.

1

Getting Started

1.1 To the Student

Welcome to the Student Edition of SIMULINK! In the last few years, SIMULINK
has become the most widely used software package for modeling and simulating dynamical systems in academia and industry. Now, The Student Edition
of SIMULINK, in combination with The Student Edition of MATLAB, makes it
practical for you to use this powerful environment on your own personal
computer in your home, dorm, or wherever you study.

SIMULINK encourages you to try things out. You can easily build models from
scratch, or take an existing model and add to it. Simulations are interactive, so
you can change parameters "on the fly" and immediately see what happens.
You have instant access to all of the analysis tools in MATLAB, so you can take
the results and analyze and visualize them. We hope that you will get a sense
of the *fun* of modeling and simulation, through an environment that encourages you to pose a question, model it, and see what happens.

With SIMULINK, you can move beyond idealized linear models to explore more
realistic nonlinear models, factoring in friction, air resistance, gear slippage,
hard stops, and the other things that describe real-world phenomena. It turns
your computer into a lab for modeling and analyzing systems that simply
wouldn't be possible or practical otherwise, whether the behavior of an automotive clutch system, the flutter of an airplane wing, the dynamics of a predator-
prey model, or the effect of the monetary supply on the economy.

It is also practical. With thousands of engineers around the world using
SIMULINK to model and solve real problems, knowledge of these tools will
serve you well, not only in your studies but also throughout your professional
career.

We hope you enjoy exploring the software.

1.1.1 What Is SIMULINK?

SIMULINK is a software package for modeling, simulating, and analyzing dynamical systems. It supports linear and nonlinear systems, modeled in continuous time, sampled time, or a hybrid of the two. Systems can be also multirate, i.e., have different parts that are sampled or updated at different rates.

For modeling, SIMULINK provides a graphical user interface (GUI) for building models as block diagrams, using click-and-drag mouse operations. With this interface, you can draw the models just as you would with pencil and paper (or as most textbooks depict them). This is a far cry from previous simulation packages that require you to formulate differential equations and difference equations in a language or program. SIMULINK includes a comprehensive block library of sinks, sources, linear and nonlinear components, and connectors. You can also customize and create your own blocks.

Models are hierarchical, so you can build models using both top-down and bottom-up approaches. You can view the system at a high-level, then double-click on blocks to go down through the levels to see increasing levels of model detail. This provides insight into how a model is organized and how its parts interact.

After you define a model, you can simulate it, using a choice of integration methods, either from the SIMULINK menus or by entering commands in MATLAB's command window. The menus are particularly convenient for interactive work, while the command-line approach is very useful for running a batch of simulations (for example, if you are doing Monte Carlo simulations or want to sweep a parameter across a range of values). Using scopes and other display blocks, you can see the simulation results while the simulation is running. In addition, you can change parameters and immediately see what happens, for "what if" exploration. The simulation results can be put in the MATLAB workspace for postprocessing and visualization.

Model analysis tools include linearization and trimming tools, which can be accessed from the MATLAB command line, plus the many tools in MATLAB and its application toolboxes. And because MATLAB and SIMULINK are integrated, you can simulate, analyze, and revise your models in either environment at any point.

1.1.2   How to Use this Manual

Because SIMULINK is graphical and interactive, we encourage you to jump right in and try it.

The manual contains seven chapters and two appendices. Chapters 2 through 5 describe important topics, providing conceptual and procedural information as appropriate. Chapters 6 and 7 provide reference information.

For a useful introduction that will help you start using SIMULINK quickly, take a look at "Running a Demo Model" in Chapter 2. Browse around the model, double-click on blocks that look interesting, and you will quickly get a sense of how SIMULINK works. If you want a quick lesson in building a model, see "Building a Simple Model" in Chapter 2.

Chapter 3 describes in detail how to build and edit a model. It also discusses how to save and print a model and provides some useful tips.

Chapter 4 describes how SIMULINK performs a simulation. It covers simulation parameters and the integration methods used for simulation, including some of the strengths and weaknesses of each method that should help you choose the appropriate method for your problem. It also discusses multirate and hybrid systems.

Chapter 5 discusses methods for creating your own blocks and using masks to customize their appearance and use.

Chapter 6 provides reference information for all SIMULINK blocks (although blocks in the Extras library are described in Appendix B).

Chapter 7 provides reference information for the simulation and analysis tools supplied with SIMULINK.

Appendix A provides tables of summary information about all block libraries (except the Extras library) provided with SIMULINK.

Appendix B provides brief descriptions of blocks in the Extras library. These are more advanced or specialized blocks and are included for their usefulness.

Although we have tried to provide the most complete and up-to-date information in this manual, some information may have changed after it was printed. Please check the README file delivered with your SIMULINK system for the latest release notes.

1.1.3 Comparing The Student Edition of SIMULINK to Professional SIMULINK

The Student Edition is available for Windows compatible personal computers and Macintosh systems. It is identical to the SIMULINK 1.3 professional version except for the following:

- Requires The Student Edition of MATLAB version 4.

- Models are limited to 40 blocks. (Note that Subsystem blocks and Inport and Outport blocks are not included in this limitation, so there is no penalty for making your model hierarchical. Some SIMULINK blocks are compound mask blocks and contain more than one block.)

- Prints to Windows, Macintosh, and PostScript printing devices only.

- Available in single-user licenses only (no networking).

- S-functions (linked C code for blocks) are not supported.

The Student Edition of SIMULINK provides a Student User Upgrade Discount for purchase of the professional version (refer to the registration card for more information).

1.1.4 How to Upgrade to Professional SIMULINK

The professional versions of MATLAB and SIMULINK are available for MS-Windows and Macintosh personal computers; UNIX workstations from Sun, Hewlett-Packard, IBM, Silicon Graphics, and Digital; and VMS computers. For product information or to place an order, call or write your educational account representative at The MathWorks at:

The MathWorks, Inc.
University Sales Department
24 Prime Park Way
Natick, Massachusetts 01760-1500
Phone: (508) 653-1415
Fax: (508) 653-2997
Email: info@mathworks.com

1.1.5   Technical Support

1.1.5.1   Student Support Policy

Neither Prentice-Hall, Inc. nor The MathWorks, Inc. provides technical support to student users of The Student Edition of SIMULINK.

If you encounter difficulty while using the Student Edition software:

1. Read the relevant tutorial and reference sections of this *User's Guide* containing information on the commands or procedures you are trying to execute.

2. Use the software's online help facility by typing `help simulink` at the MATLAB prompt.

3. Write down the sequence of procedures you were executing so that you can explain the nature of the problem to your instructor. Be certain to note the exact error message you encountered.

4. If you have consulted this *User's Guide* and the online help and are still stymied, you can post your question to the `comp.soft-sys.matlab` newsgroup, if you have access to Usenet newsgroups. Many active SIMULINK users participate in the newsgroup, and they are a good resource for answers or tips about using SIMULINK.

1.1.5.2   Student User Registration

Students who have purchased the software package will find a card in the package for registering as a user of The Student Edition of SIMULINK. Take a moment now to complete and return this card to us. Registered student users:

• Are entitled to replace defective disks at no charge.

• Qualify for a discount on upgrades to professional versions of SIMULINK.

• Receive the *MATLAB News & Notes* quarterly newsletter, with information on new products, technical notes and tips, application articles, a calendar of trade shows and conferences, and other useful information.

• Become active members of the worldwide SIMULINK user community.

1.1.5.3   Defective Disk Replacement

Contact Prentice Hall at (201) 592-3096 for disk replacement. You must send Prentice Hall your damaged or defective disk, and they will provide you with a new one.

1.1.5.4 Limited Warranty

No warranties, express or implied, are made by The MathWorks, Inc. that the program or documentation is free of error. Further, The MathWorks, Inc. does not warrant the program for correctness, accuracy, or fitness for a task. You rely on the results of the program solely at your own risk. The program should not be relied on as the sole basis to solve a problem whose incorrect solution could result in injury to person or property. If the program is employed in such a manner, it is at the user's own risk, and The MathWorks, Inc. disclaims all liability for such misuse. Neither The MathWorks, Inc. nor anyone else who has been involved in the creation, production, or delivery of this program shall be liable for any direct or indirect damages.

1.2 Professional Application Toolboxes

One of the key features of SIMULINK is that it is built atop MATLAB. As a result, SIMULINK users have direct access to the wide range of MATLAB-based tools for generating, analyzing, and optimizing systems implemented in SIMULINK. These tools include MATLAB Application Toolboxes, specialized collections of M-files for working on particular classes of problems.

Toolboxes are more than just collections of useful functions; they represent the efforts of some of the world's top researchers in fields such as controls, signal processing, and system identification. Because of this, the MATLAB Application Toolboxes let you "stand on the shoulders" of world class scientists.

All toolboxes are built using MATLAB. This has some very important implications for you:

- Every toolbox builds on the robust numerics, rock-solid accuracy, and years of experience in MATLAB.

- You get seamless and immediate integration with SIMULINK and any other toolboxes you may own.

- Since all toolboxes are written in MATLAB code, you can take advantage of MATLAB's open-system approach. You can inspect M-files, add to them, or use them for templates when you're creating your own functions.

- Every toolbox is available on any computer platform that runs MATLAB.

The Student Edition of MATLAB contains two toolboxes, bundled free with the software: the Signals and Systems Toolbox and the Symbolic Math Toolbox. These toolboxes are educational versions of the professional Signal Processing Toolbox, Control System Toolbox, and Symbolic Math Toolbox.

Here is a list of professional toolboxes currently available from The Math-Works. This list is by no means static—there are more being created every year.

The Control System Toolbox

The Control System Toolbox, the foundation of the MATLAB control design toolbox family, contains functions for modeling, analyzing, and designing automatic control systems. The application of automatic control grows with each year as sensors and computers get cheaper. As a result, automatic controllers are used not only in highly technical settings for automotive and aerospace systems, computer peripherals, and process control, but also in less obvious applications such as washing machines and cameras.

The Frequency-Domain System Identification Toolbox

The Frequency-Domain System Identification Toolbox by István Kollár, in cooperation with Johan Schoukens and researchers at the Vrije Universiteit in Brussels, is a set of M-files for modeling linear systems based on measurements of the system's frequency response.

The Fuzzy Logic Toolbox

The Fuzzy Logic Toolbox provides a complete set of GUI-based tools for designing, simulating, and analyzing fuzzy inference systems. Fuzzy logic provides an easily understandable, yet powerful way to map an input space to an output space with arbitrary complexity, with rules and relationships specified in natural language. Systems can be simulated in MATLAB or incorporated into a SIMULINK block diagram, with the ability to generate code for standalone execution.

The Higher-Order Spectral Analysis Toolbox

The Higher-Order Spectral Analysis Toolbox, by Jerry Mendel, C. L. (Max) Nikias, and Ananthram Swami, provides tools for signal processing using higher-order spectra. These methods are particularly useful for analyzing signals originating from a nonlinear process or corrupted by non-Gaussian noise.

The Image Processing Toolbox

The Image Processing Toolbox contains tools for image processing and algorithm development. It includes tools for filter design and image restoration; image enhancement; analysis and statistics; color, geometric, and morphological operations; and 2-D transforms.

The Model Predictive Control Toolbox

The Model Predictive Control Toolbox was written by Manfred Morari and N. Lawrence Ricker. Model predictive control is especially useful for control applications with many input and output variables, many of which have constraints. As a result, it has become particularly popular in chemical engineering and other process control applications.

The Mu-Analysis and Synthesis Toolbox

The Mu-Analysis and Synthesis Toolbox, by Gary Balas, Andy Packard, John Doyle, Keith Glover, and Roy Smith, contains specialized tools for H_∞ optimal control, and μ-analysis and synthesis, an approach to advanced robust control design of multivariable linear systems.

The NAG Foundation Toolbox

The NAG Foundation Toolbox includes over 200 numeric computation functions from the well-regarded NAG Fortran subroutine libraries. It provides specialized tools for boundary-value problems, optimization, adaptive quadrature, surface and curve-fitting, and other applications.

The Neural Network Toolbox

The Neural Network Toolbox by Howard Demuth and Mark Beale is a collection of MATLAB functions for designing and simulating neural networks. Neural networks are computing architectures, inspired by biological nervous systems, that are useful in applications where formal analysis is extremely difficult or impossible, such as pattern recognition and nonlinear system identification and control.

The Nonlinear Control Design Toolbox

The Nonlinear Control Design Toolbox is an add-on to SIMULINK. It allows the design of linear and nonlinear control systems, using a time-domain based optimization technique. It includes a GUI for drawing performance constraints and tuning controller parameters.

The Optimization Toolbox

The Optimization Toolbox contains commands for the optimization of general linear and nonlinear functions, including those with constraints. An optimization problem can be visualized as trying to find the lowest (or highest) point in a complex, highly contoured landscape. An optimization algorithm can thus be likened to an explorer wandering through valleys and across plains in search of the topological extremes.

The Quantitative Feedback Theory Toolbox

The Quantitative Feedback Theory Toolbox by Yossi Chait, Craig Borghesani, and Oded Yaniv implements QFT, a frequency-domain approach to controller design for uncertain systems that provides direct insight into the trade-offs between controller complexity (hence the ability to implement it) and specifications.

The Robust Control Toolbox

The Robust Control Toolbox provides a specialized set of tools for the analysis and synthesis of control systems that are "robust" with respect to uncertainties that can arise in the real world. The Robust Control Toolbox was created by controls theorists Richard Y. Chiang and Michael G. Safonov.

The Signal Processing Toolbox

The Signal Processing Toolbox contains tools for signal processing. Applications include audio (e.g., compact disc and digital audio tape), video (digital HDTV, image processing, and compression), telecommunications (fax and voice telephone), medicine (CAT scan, magnetic resonance imaging), geophysics, and econometrics.

SIMULINK Real-Time Workshop™

The SIMULINK Real-Time Workshop is an add-on to SIMULINK for rapid prototyping, real-time simulation, and implementing control strategies on real-time hardware. It provides code generation of SIMULINK block diagrams and templates for real-time operating systems and various hardware environments.

The Spline Toolbox

The Spline Toolbox by Carl de Boor, a pioneer in the field of splines, provides a set of M-files for constructing and using splines, which are piecewise polynomial approximations. Splines are useful because they can approximate other functions without the nasty side-effects that result from other kinds of approximations, such as piecewise linear curves.

The Statistics Toolbox

The Statistics Toolbox provides a set of M-files for statistical data analysis, modeling, and Monte Carlo simulation, with GUI-based tools for exploring fundamental concepts in statistics and probability.

The Symbolic Math Toolbox

The Symbolic Math Toolbox gives MATLAB an integrated set of tools for symbolic computation and variable-precision arithmetic, based on Maple V®. The Extended Symbolic Math Toolbox adds support for Maple programming plus additional specialized functions.

The System Identification Toolbox

The System Identification Toolbox, written by Lennart Ljung, is a collection of tools for estimation and identification. System identification is a way to find a mathematical model for a physical system (like an electric motor, or even a financial market) based only on a record of the system's inputs and outputs.

1.3 SIMULINK for Windows

1.3.1 System Requirements

SIMULINK for Windows has the same system requirements as MATLAB. The Windows version of The Student Edition of SIMULINK requires:

- The Student Edition of MATLAB version 4 for Microsoft Windows
- A personal computer with an Intel (or compatible) 80386, 80486, or Pentium processor
- MS-DOS version 3.1 or later
- Microsoft Windows version 3.1 or later
- 8 MB of extended memory
- 15 MB of free disk space on your hard drive
- High-density 3 ½" floppy disk drive
- Microsoft Windows-supported mouse and monitor

These items are strongly recommended:

- A math coprocessor (if not already installed)
- Additional memory
- 8-bit graphics adapter and display (for 256 simultaneous colors)
- Microsoft Windows-supported graphics accelerator card
- Microsoft Windows-supported printer
- Microsoft Windows-supported sound card

1.3.2 Installing SIMULINK for Windows

The Student Edition of SIMULINK for Windows ships on a single high-density 3 1/2" disk.

Please be sure that Windows and The Student Edition of MATLAB version 4 are installed and running properly before attempting to install The Student Edition of SIMULINK.

When you are ready to install SIMULINK, follow these steps:

1. Start Windows.

2. Insert the SIMULINK distribution disk into your disk drive.

3. When the Windows Program Manager is displayed, select the **Run** option on the **File** menu.

4. At the **Command line** prompt, enter a:setup (or b:setup, if appropriate), and click on the **OK** button.

5. At the **Directory** prompt, enter the name of the directory into which you want to install SIMULINK, and click on the **OK** button. The default is C:\MATLAB, but you can specify another drive and/or directory.

The installation takes a few minutes while the program and other files are decompressed. During the installation, information is displayed about the amount of disk space used and the percent of installation that is complete.

After installation, your \MATLAB\TOOLBOX\SIMULINK directory contains the following subdirectories:

\SIMULINK	SIMULINK M-files
\BLOCKS	SIMULINK block library, extra blocks, and a help file
\SIMDEMOS	SIMULINK demonstration M-files

1.4 SIMULINK for Macintosh

1.4.1 System Requirements

SIMULINK for the Macintosh has the same system requirements as MATLAB. The Macintosh version of The Student Edition of SIMULINK requires:

• The Student Edition of MATLAB version 4 for Macintosh

• A Macintosh equipped with a 68030, 68040, or PowerPC processor

• 15 MB of free space on your hard drive

- 8 MB memory partition for MATLAB (at least 12 MB total system memory)
- A SuperDrive (1.4 MB) floppy disk drive
- Color QuickDraw
- System 6.0.5 with 32-bit QuickDraw installed, or System 6.0.7 or later
- A 12" or larger monitor

These items are strongly recommended:

- Floating-point unit (for 68030- and 68040-based Macintosh)
- System 7 or later
- Additional memory
- 8-bit graphics capability and display (for 256 simultaneous colors)
- Apple LaserWriter or other PostScript printer
- Suggested total system memory assumes a reasonably large System Folder. Your memory requirements may vary depending upon the exact size of your System Folder.

1.4.2 Installing SIMULINK for Macintosh

The Student Edition of SIMULINK for the Macintosh ships on a single high-density 3 $\frac{1}{2}$" disk, which is labeled **SIMULINK**.

Please be sure that The Student Edition of MATLAB version 4 is installed and running properly before installing The Student Edition of SIMULINK.

When you are ready to install SIMULINK, follow these steps:

1. Insert the SIMULINK distribution disk into your floppy disk drive, and double-click on it to open it.

2. Drag the Student SIMULINK 1 Installer file onto your hard disk, and eject the disk.

3. SIMULINK is shipped in compressed form and must be decompressed before it can be used. To decompress the software, double-click on the Student SIMULINK 1 Installer file on your hard disk. An **Open File** dialog box appears with the prompt "Install software into folder:"

4. Locate and open the Student Edition of MATLAB toolbox folder, so that the names of the local, matlab, sigsys, and symbolic folders are listed in the dialog box; then click on the **Install** button. A thermometer displays the progress of the decompression process. When the process is complete, a new simulink folder appears in the selected location.

5. Delete the Student SIMULINK 1 Installer file from your hard disk.

6. When you are done, store the disk as a backup copy.

After installation, your `Student Edition of MATLAB:Toolbox:simulink` folder contains the following folders:

`simulink`	SIMULINK M-files
`blocks`	SIMULINK block library, extra blocks, and a help file
`simdemos`	SIMULINK demonstration M-files

2
Quick Start

This chapter shows you how to start using SIMULINK by running a demonstration model and building a simple model of your own.

2.1 Running a Demo Model

An interesting demo program provided with SIMULINK models the thermodynamics of a house. To run this demo, follow these steps.

1. Start the Student Edition of MATLAB by double-clicking on the MATLAB icon.

2. Start SIMULINK by entering `simulink` in the command window. The SIMULINK Block Library window appears.

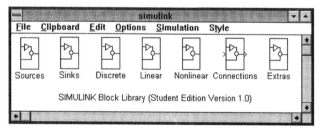

3. Access the demo by opening the Extras library. Do this by double-clicking on the Extras library icon, at the right side of the block library window. Open the Demos sublibrary, then double-click on the House Thermostat box. SIMULINK creates a new window and displays the model in the window. SIMULINK also opens two Scope blocks.

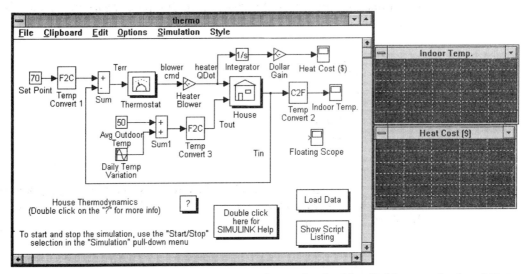

4. Load the data used in the simulation by double-clicking on the Load Data block near the bottom right corner of the model.

5. To start the simulation, pull down the **Simulation** menu and choose the **Start** command. SIMULINK displays the house temperature output in the Indoor Temp Scope block and the cumulative heating cost output in the Heat Cost Scope block.

6. To stop the simulation, pull down the **Simulation** menu again and choose the **Stop** command.

7. Close the model by choosing **Close** on the **File** menu.

2.1.1 Description of the Demo

The demo models the thermodynamics of a house using a simple model. The thermostat is set to 70 degrees Fahrenheit and is affected by the outside temperature, which varies by applying a sine wave with amplitude of 15 degrees to a base temperature of 50 degrees.

The internal and external temperatures are fed into the House subsystem, which updates the internal temperature. Double-click on the House block to see the blocks it contains.

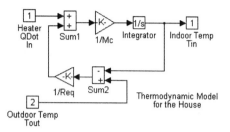

The Thermostat subsystem models the operation of a thermostat, determining when the heating system is turned on and off. Double-click on the block to see the blocks it contains.

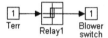

Both the outside and inside temperatures are converted from Fahrenheit to Centigrade by subsystems:

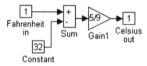

When the heat is on, the heating costs are computed and displayed on the Heat Cost ($) Scope block. The internal temperature is displayed on the Indoor Temp Scope block.

2.1.2   Some Things to Try

Here are several things to try to see how the model responds to different parameters.

- Open the Floating Scope block. Floating scopes allow you to examine the signal passing through any selected line. To see how this block works, start the simulation, then select different lines to see their signals displayed on the scope.

- Enlarge a Scope block to see how you can modify its parameters. The block contains a signal display area and controls that enable you to select the range of the signal displayed. The horizontal axis represents time and the vertical axis represents the signal value.

- The block labeled Set Point (at the top left of the model) sets the desired internal temperature. Open this block and reset the value to 80 degrees while the simulation is running. See how the indoor temperature and heating costs differ. Alternatively, adjust the outside temperature and see how it affects the simulation.

- Adjust the daily temperature variation by opening the block labeled Daily Temp Variation and changing the amplitude. Rerun the simulation and observe the differences.

2.1.3 What this Demo Illustrates

This demo illustrates several tasks commonly used when building models:

- Running the simulation involves specifying parameters and starting the simulation with the **Start** command. Specifying simulation parameters and running the simulation are described in detail in Chapter 4.

- Subsystems (such as the Thermostat, House, and temperature conversion blocks) can be used to "hide" complex groups of blocks behind a subsystem block. Open each subsystem; SIMULINK displays its underlying blocks in a new window. Creating subsystems is described in detail in Chapter 3.

- Scope blocks display graphic output much as an oscilloscope does. Scope blocks display the output of the block driving it. The floating Scope block, which is not connected to any blocks in the model, enables you to monitor the signal on any selected line. Scope blocks are described in Chapter 6.

- Several block parameters are defined by workspace variables. These variables are assigned values by loading data into the workspace using the Load Data subsystem, which uses the `eval` command to define the variables by invoking the `thermdat.m` M-file.

2.2 Other Useful Demos

Other demos in the Extras library illustrate useful modeling concepts. For example, the Inverted Pendulum with Animation demo contains three masked blocks that are worth examining. Masking allows you to create customized icons for blocks. It also lets you design a dialog box for a block (you enter a block's parameters on its dialog box).

Examine the masking on some masked blocks. The Pendulum subsystem, the Discrete State Estimator subsystem, and the Animation block are masked blocks. Select one, then choose **Mask** on the **Options** menu. See how the mask handles parameters for the underlying blocks and, for the Animation block, customizes its icon. Masking is described in detail in Chapter 5.

2.3 Building a Simple Model

If SIMULINK is not running, start it by following the steps described earlier in this chapter.

To create a new model, choose **New** on the **File** menu. SIMULINK creates a new window. You might want to move the window to the top right of your screen so you can see its contents and the contents of block libraries at the same time.

Open the Sources library by double-clicking on the Sources icon. SIMULINK displays a window that contains all the blocks in the Sources library; these blocks are signal sources. The Sources library window looks like this:

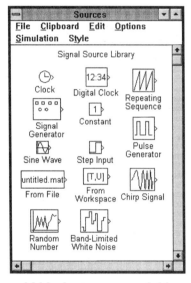

You add blocks to your model by copying them from a block library or from another model. For this exercise, you'll need to copy the Signal Generator block from the Sources library.

To copy the Signal Generator block from the Sources block library, click on the Signal Generator block and drag it into your model window. When you release the mouse button, SIMULINK displays the block icon.

You can view a block's parameters by double-clicking on the block and examining the dialog block that appears. Try it with the Signal Generator block. You'll see a dialog box like this one (for Windows systems):

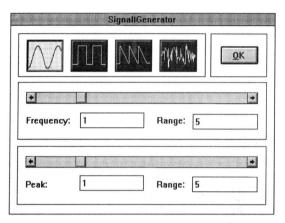

Here's how this dialog box looks on a Macintosh:

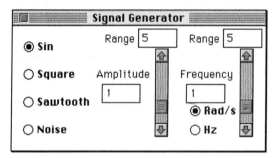

This dialog box shows the waveforms you can choose and the controls for specifying the amplitude and frequency of the signal generated by the block. Change the value displayed in the **Frequency** field to 6. If you're using a PC, click on the **OK** button to accept the value and close the dialog box. If you're using a Macintosh, close the dialog box.

Now, copy the Scope block (from the Sinks library) into your model, to the right of the Signal Generator block. Your model should look something like this:

Double-click on the Scope block to open it. You'll notice that the Scope block is a graphic representation of an oscilloscope.

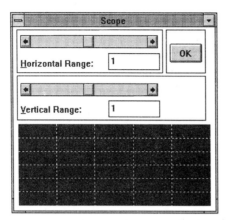

Move the Scope window to a convenient location. Change the value in the **Horizontal Range** field, which represents time, to 10.

Now connect these blocks. To connect the blocks, position the pointer on the Signal Generator's output port, hold down the mouse button, drag the pointer either to the Scope's input port or over the Scope block itself; then release the mouse button. SIMULINK draws a connecting line between the blocks. If the connecting line is not straight, you can move either block up or down. The connecting line uses an arrow to show the direction of the signal flow.

When you are satisfied with your model, you can start the simulation. To select the integration algorithm and parameters to be used during the simulation, choose **Parameters** on the **Simulation** menu. SIMULINK displays the **Control Panel** dialog box. The **Control Panel** dialog box for Windows appears below:

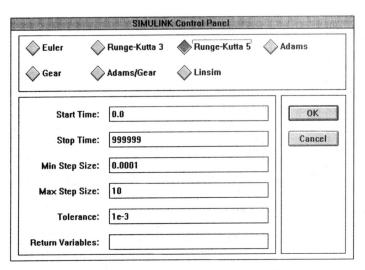

Change the **Maximum Step Size** parameter to 0.01. All other parameter values are acceptable, as is the default integration algorithm (Runge-Kutta 5). **Click on the OK** button to close the dialog box. Start the simulation by choosing **Start** on the **Simulation** menu.

If the Scope block's window is not open, double-click on the block to open it. **The** Signal Generator outputs *sin(6t)* for each time step and the Scope shows its input as the trace of the sine wave.

The controls in the Scope and Signal Generator blocks' windows are active during the simulation. You can select a different waveform on the Signal Generator and see immediate results on the Scope. Move the sliders or **change** the values for the Signal Generator and the Scope to see how they affect **the** display.

The simulation stops when it reaches the stop-time specified in the **Control Panel** dialog box or when you choose **Stop** on the **Simulation** menu.

To exit SIMULINK, either choose **Exit MATLAB** on the **File** menu (**Quit on the** Macintosh) or type quit in the MATLAB command window.

3

Creating a Model

This chapter discusses the tasks and procedures useful in building SIMULINK models. It includes these topics:

- SIMULINK windows and menus
- A model-building exercise
- Building a model
- Saving a model
- Printing a block diagram
- Tips for building models

3.1 SIMULINK Windows and Menus

To start SIMULINK, you must first start MATLAB. At the MATLAB prompt, enter the simulink command. Your desktop includes the MATLAB command window and the SIMULINK Block Library window, shown below.

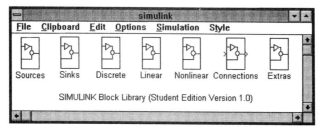

The SIMULINK Block Library window displays icons for its block libraries. You build models by copying blocks from block libraries into a model window. The block libraries and all blocks are described in Chapter 6. The SIMULINK Block

Library and the other block libraries accessible from this window are all SIMULINK models, drawn with no blocks connected.

When you run a simulation and analyze its results, you can use MATLAB commands, which you enter in the MATLAB command window. Running a simulation and analyzing its results are discussed in Chapter 4.

SIMULINK uses separate windows to display a block library, a model, or graphical (scope) simulation output. These windows are not MATLAB figure windows and cannot be manipulated using MATLAB Handle Graphics commands.

SIMULINK windows are sized to accommodate the most common screen resolutions available. However, if you have a monitor with exceptionally high or low resolution, you may find the window sizes too large or too small. You can resize the window by dragging on the borders, then choosing the **Save** command on the **File** menu to preserve the new window dimensions.

You access SIMULINK commands from the SIMULINK menus.

- On Windows systems, a SIMULINK menu bar appears near the top of each SIMULINK window. The menu commands apply to the contents of that window.

- On Macintosh systems, the SIMULINK menu bar appears at the top of the desktop. The menu commands apply to the contents of the active window.

A common mistake for new SIMULINK users is to start a simulation while the SIMULINK Block Library is the active window. Make sure your model window is the active window before starting a simulation.

You terminate a SIMULINK session by choosing:

- **Exit MATLAB** on the **File** menu (on a Windows system).

- **Quit** on the **File** menu (on a Macintosh system).

3.2 A Model-Building Exercise

This example shows you how to build a model using many of the model building commands and actions you will use to build your own models. The instructions that describe the actions used to build this model are concise. All of the tasks are described in more detail later in this chapter.

The model generates a sine wave using a Signal Generator block. It scales a copy of the waveform by passing it through a Gain block. Both the original and the scaled signals are combined into a vector signal using a **Mux** block. That signal is displayed using a Scope block and sent to a workspace variable. **The** block diagram of the model looks like this:

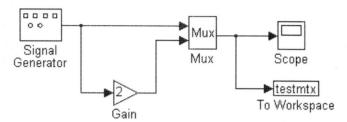

In this model, you get blocks from these libraries:

• Sources library (for the Signal Generator block)

• Linear library (for the Gain block)

• Connections library (for the Mux block)

• Sinks library (for the Scope and the To Workspace blocks)

Create a new model window by selecting **New** on the **File** menu.

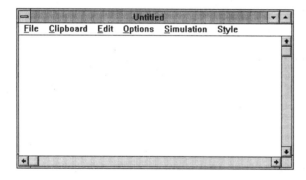

Open the Sources library to copy the Signal Generator block.

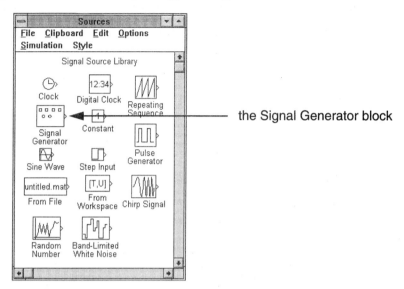

the Signal Generator block

To copy a block from its block library, drag the block into the model window. To do this, position the cursor over the Signal Generator block, then press and hold down the mouse button. See how the cursor shape changes.

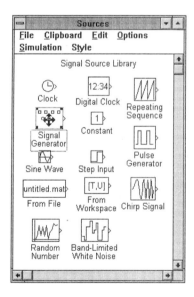

Now, drag the block into the model window (called Untitled). As you move the block, you see the outline of the block and its name move with the pointer.

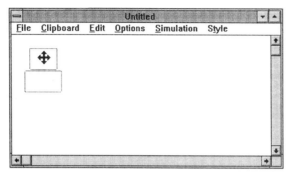

When the pointer is in the model window, release the mouse button. A copy of the Signal Generator block is now in your model window.

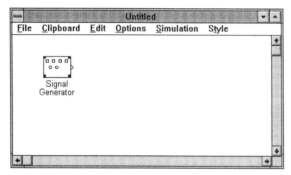

In the same way, copy the rest of the blocks into the model window. You can move a block from one place in the model window to another using the same dragging technique you used to copy the block.

You might have noticed that the Mux block has three input ports but only two input signals. To adjust the number of input ports, open the Mux block by double-clicking on it. SIMULINK displays its dialog box. Change the **Number of inputs** parameter value to 2, then click on the **OK** button. SIMULINK adjusts the number of input ports.

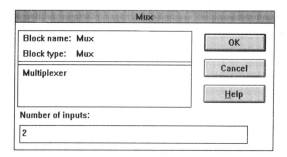

With all the blocks copied into the model window, the **model should look something** like this:

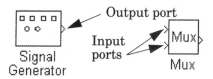

Now connect the blocks. If you examine the block icons, you see **an angle** bracket on the right of the Signal Generator block and two on the left of the Mux block. The > symbol pointing out of a block is an output port; if the symbol points to a block, it is an input port. When the blocks are connected, the port symbols disappear.

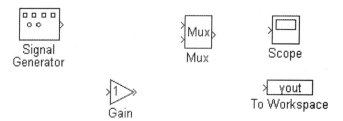

Connect the Signal Generator block to the Mux block. Position the pointer over the output port on the right side of the Signal Generator block.

Press and hold down the mouse button. Notice that the cursor changes to a cross hairs shape.

While continuing to hold down the mouse button, move the cursor to the top input port of the Mux block or over the Mux block itself. Notice that the cursor keeps its cross hairs shape and that a line connects the Signal Generator block to the top (first available) input port of the Mux block.

Now release the mouse button. The blocks are connected.

If you look again at the model at the beginning of this section, you'll notice that most of the lines connect output ports of blocks to input ports of other blocks. However, two lines connect *lines* to input ports of other blocks. These lines connect the Signal Generator output to the Gain block, and the Mux output to the To Workspace block and carry the same signal as the lines from which they originate. In other words, the Signal Generator outputs the same signal to the Mux block and the Gain block, and the Mux block outputs the same signal to the Scope block and the To Workspace block.

Drawing this kind of line is slightly different than drawing the line you just drew. To weld a connection to an existing line, follow these steps. First, position the cursor *on the line* between the Signal Generator and the Mux block.

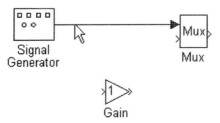

While pressing the mouse button, press and hold down the **Ctrl** key on a Windows system, or the **Option** key on a Macintosh. Drag the cursor to the input port of the Gain block or over the Gain block itself.

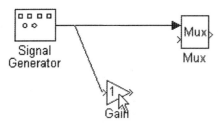

Now, release the mouse button. SIMULINK draws a line between the starting point and the Gain input port.

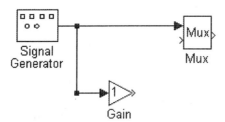

Now you can draw a similar line between the Mux output line and the To Workspace block. Finish making connections.

When you're finished connecting the blocks, you need to adjust some of the block parameters. First, open the Gain block and change the **Gain** parameter to 2.

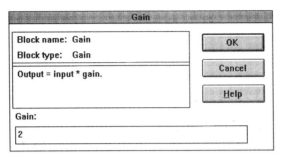

Next, open the To Workspace block and change the **Variable name** parameter to testmtx. This is the name of the workspace variable that will hold the simulation output.

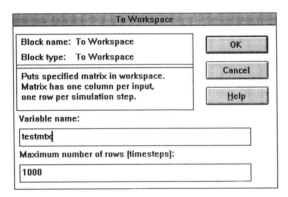

The default output of the Signal Generator block is a sine wave with an amplitude of 1. Because that's acceptable for this exercise, there's no need to change any parameters for that block. You might find it interesting to open that block to see the other waveforms it generates.

Run the simulation for 10 seconds. First, set the simulation parameters by choosing **Parameters** on the **Simulation** menu. On the dialog box that appears (the Windows version, called the **Control Panel** dialog box, appears below), adjust the **Stop Time** to 10 and change the **Maximum Step Size** to 0.1.

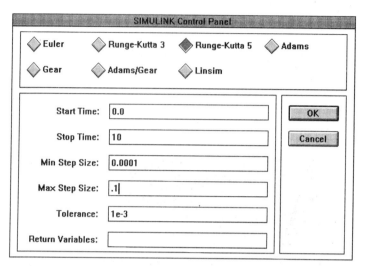

Now, open the Scope block to view the simulation output. Before you start the simulation, adjust the parameters so you can view the entire simulation. Change the **Horizontal Range** (time) to 10 (seconds) and change the **Vertical Range** (which, for this simulation, corresponds to the sine wave amplitude) to 3.

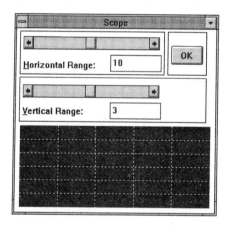

Keeping the Scope window open, run the simulation. Choose **Start** on the **Simulation** menu and watch the traces of the Scope block's vector input.

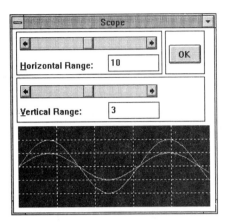

To save this model, choose **Save** on the **File** menu and specify the name and location of the M-file that describes the model. To terminate SIMULINK and MATLAB, choose **Exit MATLAB** (on a Windows system) or **Quit** (on a Macintosh system) on the **File** menu.

This exercise showed you how to perform the most common model-building tasks. These and other tasks are described in more detail in the rest of this chapter.

3.3   Building a Model

This section discusses tasks involved in constructing your model.

To create a new model, choose the **New** command on the **File** menu. SIMULINK creates a new window. You can move the window as you do other windows.

To edit an existing model diagram, either

- Choose the **Open** command on the **File** menu, then specify the M-file that describes the model you want to edit, or
- Enter the name of the model in the MATLAB command window.

SIMULINK creates a new window and displays that model in the window.

3.3.1 Selecting Objects

Many model building and editing actions require that you first **select one or more blocks and lines (objects)**.

3.3.1.1 Selecting One Object

To select an object, click on it. Small "handles" appear at the corners of the object. For example, the figure below shows a selected Sine Wave block and a selected line:

When you select an object by clicking on it, any other selected objects become deselected.

3.3.1.2 Selecting More than One Object

You can select more than one object either by selecting objects one at a time or by selecting objects located near each other using a bounding box.

3.3.1.2.1 Selecting Objects One at a Time

To select more than one object by selecting each object individually, hold down the **Shift** key and click on each object to be selected. To deselect a selected object, click on the object again, while holding down the **Shift** key.

3.3.1.2.2 Selecting Objects Using a Bounding Box

An easy way to select more than one object in the same area of the window is to draw a bounding box around the objects. To define the bounding box:

1. Define the starting corner of a bounding box by positioning the pointer at one corner of the box, then pressing (and holding down) the mouse button.

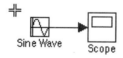

2. Drag the pointer to the opposite corner of the box.

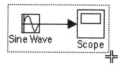

3. Release the mouse button. All blocks and lines at least partially enclosed by the bounding box are selected.

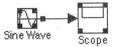

3.3.1.2.3   Selecting the Entire Model

To select all objects in the active window, choose **Select All** on the **Edit** menu.

3.3.2   Manipulating Blocks

This section discusses how to perform useful model building actions involving blocks.

3.3.2.1   Copying and Moving Blocks from One Window to Another

As you build your model, you will often copy blocks from SIMULINK block libraries or other model windows into your model window. To do this, follow these steps:

1. Open the appropriate block library or source model window.

2. Drag the block you want to copy into your target model window. To drag a block, position the cursor over the block icon, then press and hold down the mouse button. Move the cursor into the model window, then release the mouse button. If you need information about selecting more than one block, see "Selecting More than One Object" on page 34.

You can also copy blocks by using the **Copy** and **Paste** commands on the **Edit** menu:

1. Select the block you want to copy.

2. Choose **Copy** on the **Edit** menu.

3. Select the model window to make it the active window.

4. Choose **Paste** on the **Edit** menu.

SIMULINK assigns a name to each copied block. If it is the first block of its type in the model, its name is the same as its name in the window from which you copied it. For example, if you copy the Gain block from the Linear library into your model window, the name of the new block is Gain. If your model already contains a block named Gain, SIMULINK adds a sequence number to the block name (for example, Gain1, Gain2, etc.). You can rename blocks; see "Manipulating Block Names" on page 39.

If you copy a block that is connected to other blocks, SIMULINK does not copy the connecting lines. If you copy connected blocks, SIMULINK also copies the connecting lines.

When you copy a block, the new block inherits all the parameter values of the original block.

SIMULINK uses an invisible five-pixel grid to simplify the alignment of objects. All objects within a model snap to a line on the grid. You can move a block a small amount up, down, left, or right by selecting the block and using the arrow keys.

You can copy or move blocks to compatible applications using the **Copy**, **Cut**, and **Paste** commands. Only the graphic representation of the blocks, not their parameters, are copied.

Moving one or more blocks from one window to another is similar to copying a block except that you hold down the **Shift** key while you select the block or blocks.

3.3.2.2 Moving Blocks in a Model

To move a single block from one place to another in a model window, select the block and drag it to a new location. SIMULINK automatically reroutes lines connected to the moved block.

To move more than one block, including connecting lines:

1. Select the blocks and lines. If you need information about how to select more than one block, see "Selecting More than One Object" on page 34.

   If you select more than one object by selecting them one at a time, don't release the mouse button after you select the last object. Otherwise, when you click on an object you already selected, that object becomes deselected.

   If you select more than one object by defining a bounding box, define the box; then click on a selected block and drag it to drag all the bounded objects. Don't click on a line – if you click on a line, only that line is selected. If you click on an unoccupied area of the model, all objects become deselected.

2. Drag the selected blocks and lines to their new location and release the mouse button.

If you move a block over an existing line, you can reroute the line by selecting it, then choosing **Reroute Lines** on the **Options** menu. SIMULINK redraws the line so that it goes around the block.

3.3.2.3   Duplicating Blocks in a Model

How you duplicate blocks in a model depends on the computer you are using:

- **Windows:** Hold down the **Ctrl** key, select the block with the left mouse button; then drag the block to a new location. You can also select the block by pressing the right mouse button while the pointer is over the block, and dragging it to a new location.

- **Macintosh:** Hold down the **Option** key, select the block; then drag it to a new location.

3.3.2.4   Specifying Block Parameters

Certain aspects of a block's function are defined by the block's parameters. You can assign values to a block's parameters by accessing the block's dialog box. Open (double-click) the block. SIMULINK displays the block's dialog box, which lists the parameters and their current values. You can change these values or accept the displayed values.

The reference pages that describe the block (in Chapter 6) show the dialog box and discuss the block's parameters.

3.3.2.5   Deleting Blocks

To delete one or more blocks, select the block(s) to be deleted and press the **Delete** key, or choose **Clear** or **Cut** from the **Edit** menu. The **Cut** command writes the block or blocks into the clipboard, making them available to be pasted into a model. Using the **Delete** key or the **Clear** command does not affect the contents of the clipboard.

3.3.2.6   Disconnecting Blocks

To disconnect a block from the model without deleting it, hold down the **Shift** key, then select and drag the block from its original position in the model. This technique is useful in converting connected Scope blocks to floating Scope blocks.

3.3.2.7   Changing the Orientation of Blocks

By default, signals flow through a block from left to right. Inputs are on the left, and outputs are on the right. You can change the orientation of a block by choosing one of these commands:

- The **Rotate** command on the **Options** menu rotates a block clockwise 90 degrees.

- The **Flip Horizontal** (on a Windows system) or **Flip** (on a Macintosh) command on the **Options** menu rotates the block 180 degrees.

- The **Orientation** command on the **Style** menu lets you choose the **orientation** of the block, either **Left to Right**, **Right to Left**, **Up**, or **Down**.

The figure below shows how SIMULINK orders ports after changing the orientation of a block using the **Rotate** and **Flip** commands. The text in the blocks indicate their orientation.

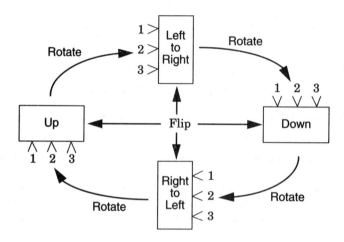

3.3.2.8   Resizing Blocks

To change the size of a block, select it, then drag any of its selection handles. The minimum size of a block is five-by-five pixels. The maximum size is limited by the size of the window. The cursor shape reflects the corner being dragged and the direction it is being dragged. While the block is being resized, a dotted rectangle shows its proposed size.

For example, the figure below shows a Signal Generator block being resized. The lower-right handle was selected and dragged to the position of the cursor. When the mouse button is released, the block assumes its new size. The figure shows what resizing looks like on a Macintosh system (the cursor shape is slightly different on a Windows system).

3.3.2.9   Manipulating Block Names

All block names in a model must be unique and must contain at least one character. By default, block names appear below blocks whose ports are on the sides, and to the right of blocks whose ports are on the top and bottom, as shown below. You can change block names and their locations.

3.3.2.9.1   Changing Block Names

You can edit block names in one of three ways:

• Select the box in which the name is displayed, then enter the new name.

• Place the insertion point in the name, then insert new text.

• Drag the mouse to select a range of text to replace, then enter the new text.

When you click the pointer on another block or take any other action, the name is accepted or rejected. If you try to change the name of a block to a name that already exists or to a name with no characters, SIMULINK displays an error message.

You can modify the font used in block names by selecting the block or blocks, then choosing a font from the **Fonts** submenu, accessible from the **Style** menu.

3.3.2.9.2   Changing the Location of a Block Name

You can change the location of a block name and whether or not it appears by choosing an option on the **Title** submenu, accessible from the **Style** menu:

• **Displayed**, the default, displays the name.

• **Hidden** does not display the name.

• **Top/Left** places the name above the block when its orientation is **Left to Right** or **Right to Left,** or to the left of the block when its orientation is **Up** or **Down**.

• **Bottom/Right**, the default, places the name below the block when its orientation is **Left to Right** or **Right to Left,** or to the right of the block when its orientation is **Up** or **Down**.

The figure below shows the position of **Top/Left** block names.

For more information about block orientation, see "Changing the Orientation of Blocks" on page 37.

3.3.2.10 Vectorization of Blocks

Almost all built-in blocks accept either scalar or vector inputs and allow you to specify scalar or vector parameters. Block descriptions in Chapter 6 discuss the characteristics of block inputs, outputs, and parameters.

You can determine which lines in a model carry vector signals by choosing the **Wide Vector Lines** option on the **Style** menu. SIMULINK draws lines that carry vectors thicker than lines that carry scalars. The figure in the next section shows wide and normal lines.

If you change your model after choosing this option, you must explicitly update the display by choosing the **Update Diagram** option on the **Style** menu. Starting the simulation also updates the display.

3.3.2.11 Scalar Expansion of Inputs and Parameters

Scalar expansion is the conversion of a scalar value into a vector of identical elements. SIMULINK applies scalar expansion to block inputs and parameters. Block descriptions in Chapter 6 indicate whether SIMULINK applies scalar expansion to inputs, parameters, or both.

3.3.2.11.1 Inputs

When using blocks with more than one input port (e.g., the Sum or Relational Operator block), you can mix vector and scalar inputs. In this case, the scalar inputs are expanded into vectors that are equal in length to the vector inputs. This example of a Sum block shows the result of expanding a scalar input to match the size of the vector block input. Note the wide vector lines.

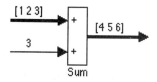

3.3.2.11.2 Parameters

You can specify the parameters for vectorized blocks as either vectors or scalars. When you specify vector parameters, each parameter element is associated with the corresponding element in the input vector(s). When you specify scalar parameters, SIMULINK applies scalar expansion to convert them automatically into appropriately sized vectors.

This example shows that a scalar parameter (the Gain) is expanded to match the size of the block input, a three-element vector.

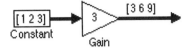

3.3.3   Manipulating Lines

Lines connect the output of a block to the input of another block. Lines also connect other lines to the input of a block. Any number of lines can be connected to an output port, but only one line can be connected to each input port. (The Mux block is useful for combining several lines into a single vector line; see Chapter 6 for more information about that block.)

3.3.3.1   Drawing Lines Between Blocks

To connect the output of one block to the input of another:

1. Position the cursor over the first block's output port. It is not necessary to position the cursor precisely on the port. You can position the cursor close to the port.

2. Press and hold down the mouse button. The cursor changes to a cross hairs shape.

3. Drag the pointer to the second block's input port. You can position the cursor on or near the port, or in the block. If you position the cursor in the block, the line is connected to the first available input port. To connect the line to a specific port, you must position the cursor on that port before releasing the mouse button.

4. Release the mouse button. SIMULINK replaces the port symbols by a connecting line with an arrow showing the direction of signal flow. You can create connecting lines either from output to input, or from input to output.

In either case, the arrow is drawn at the appropriate input port, and the signal is the same.

3.3.3.1.1 Routing Lines Around Blocks

SIMULINK automatically routes lines around blocks rather than through them. You can, instead, direct SIMULINK to draw a line exactly as you specify it by either holding down the **Shift** key while drawing the line, drawing the line from input port to output port, or drawing a sequence of line segments.

The **Reroute Lines** option is useful for cleaning up cluttered areas of your block diagram. Using the bounding box, select an area of the model, then choose **Reroute Lines** on the **Options** menu.

3.3.3.1.2 Drawing Lines from Other Lines

You can add a line that starts from any point on an existing line. Both lines deliver the same signal to their outputs.

For example, in the following figure the diagram on the left shows a single line coming from the Product block to the Scope block. The diagram on the right shows an additional line coming from the Product block to the To Workspace block. The same signal goes to each block.

To add a line from another line, follow these steps:

1. Position the pointer on the line where you want the new line to start.

2. While holding down the **Ctrl** key (on a Windows system) or the **Option** key (on a Macintosh), press and hold down the mouse button.

3. Drag the pointer to the target port, then release the mouse button and the **Ctrl** or **Option** key. SIMULINK creates a new line between the starting and ending points.

On a Windows system, you can also use the right mouse button instead of holding down the **Ctrl** key while using the left mouse button.

3.3.3.1.3 Drawing a Line Segment

To draw a line segment, you draw a line that ends in an unoccupied area of the diagram. An arrow appears on the unconnected end of the line. To add another line segment, press the mouse button while the pointer is over the arrow and repeat the procedure.

You can use this technique to draw a line with segments exactly where you want them or to draw lines before copying blocks to which the lines are connected. When you start a simulation, SIMULINK provides a warning message if your model has any unconnected lines.

The figure below shows an unconnected line segment.

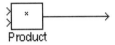

3.3.3.1.4 Line Angles

SIMULINK draws connecting lines at multiples of 45 degrees with these exceptions:

- If the pointer moves near an available port, the line snaps to that port.
- If you create a line while holding down the **Shift** key, SIMULINK draws the line as you create it.
- If you create a line by moving the pointer over the block and releasing it, the line snaps to the top-most or left-most unused port on the block.

3.3.3.2 Deleting Lines

To delete one or more lines, select the line or lines to be removed and press the **Delete** key, or choose **Clear** or **Cut** on the **Edit** menu.

3.3.3.3 Moving Line Segments

To move a line segment, follow these steps:

1. Position the pointer on the segment.

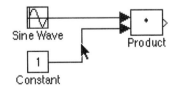

2. Press and hold down the mouse button.

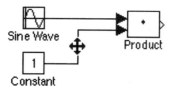

3. Drag the pointer to the desired location.

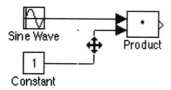

4. Release the mouse button.

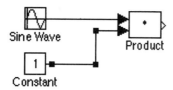

You cannot move the segments connected directly to block ports.

3.3.3.4   Moving Vertices

To move a vertex of a line, position the pointer on the vertex, press and hold down the mouse button, drag the pointer to the desired location, then release the mouse button. You cannot move the vertices at either end of the line.

The figure below shows the cursor shape and movement of the vertex as you drag it. You can drag the vertex in any direction.

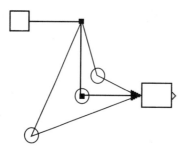

3.3.3.5   Dividing a Line into Segments

You can divide a line into two segments (or a line segment into two **segments**), leaving the ends of the line in their original locations. SIMULINK creates **line** segments and a vertex that joins them. To divide a line into **segments**, follow these steps:

1. Position the pointer on the line where you want the vertex.

2. While holding down the **Shift** key, press and hold down the **mouse button**. On a Windows system, instead of using the **Shift** key, you **can hold down** both mouse buttons.

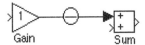

3. Drag the pointer to the desired location.

4. Release the mouse button and the **Shift** key.

3.3.4   Summary of Mouse and Keyboard Actions

This table summarizes the use of the mouse and keyboard to manipulate **blocks** and lines.

Model Building Action	Windows	Macintosh
Select object	Left mouse button	Mouse button
Select more than one object	**Shift** + left mouse button	**Shift** + mouse button
Copy object from another window	Select object and drag	Select object and drag
Move object	Select object and drag	Select object and drag

Model Building Action	Windows	Macintosh
Duplicate object	**Ctrl** + left mouse button, then drag; or right mouse button and drag	**Option** + mouse button, then drag
Connect blocks	Left mouse button	Mouse button
Disconnect block	**Shift** + drag block	**Shift** + drag block
Route lines around blocks	**Shift** + draw line	**Shift** + draw line
Draw line from another line	**Ctrl** + drag line	**Option** + drag line
Move line segment	Select segment and drag	Select segment and drag
Move vertex	Select vertex and drag	Select vertex and drag
Divide line into segments	**Shift** + drag line	**Shift** + drag line

3.3.5   Adding Text Annotations to the Model Diagram

You can add text to the model diagram by positioning the pointer where you want the text, clicking the mouse button, then typing the text. SIMULINK centers the text slightly below where you clicked the mouse button. The text must be unique in the model. Adding text is useful for labeling lines or naming and dating the model.

You can modify the font used in text annotations by selecting the text using a bounding box, then choosing a font from the **Fonts** submenu, accessible from the **Style** menu. If you need information about how to use a bounding box, see "Selecting Objects Using a Bounding Box" on page 34.

3.3.6   Creating Subsystems

As your model increases in size and complexity, you can simplify it by grouping blocks into subsystems. Grouping is useful for a number of reasons:

- It helps reduce the number of blocks displayed in your model window.
- It allows you to keep functionally related blocks together.
- It enables you to establish a hierarchical block diagram (where the subsystem blocks are on one layer and the subsystems on another).

You can create a subsystem in two ways: first, by adding a Subsystem block to your model, then adding the blocks it contains; second, by adding the blocks that make up the subsystem, then grouping those blocks into a subsystem.

To create a subsystem before adding the blocks it contains, you add a Subsystem block, then create the blocks that make up the subsystem:

1. Copy the Subsystem block from the Connections library into your model.

2. Open the Subsystem block by double-clicking on it.

3. In the empty Subsystem window, create the subsystem. Use Inport blocks to represent input from outside the subsystem and Outport blocks to represent external output. For example, the Sum block below is the only block in a subsystem. The diagram below shows the block and its Inport and Outport blocks:

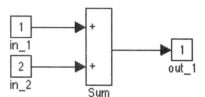

If you have already created the blocks you want to convert to a subsystem:

1. Enclose the blocks and connecting lines you want to include in the subsystem within a bounding box. For more information, see "Selecting Objects Using a Bounding Box" on page 34. You cannot specify the blocks to be grouped by selecting them individually. For example, the figure below shows a model that represents a counter. The Sum and Unit Delay blocks are selected within a bounding box:

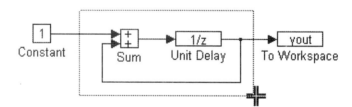

When you release the mouse button, the two blocks and all the connecting lines are selected.

2. Choose **Group** on the **Options** menu. SIMULINK replaces the blocks in the group with a single Subsystem block. The figure below shows the model after choosing the **Group** command:

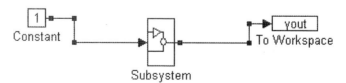

As with all blocks, you can change name of the Subsystem block. Also, you can customize the icon and dialog box for the block, using a SIMULINK feature called masking. See Chapter 5 for more information.

If you double-click on the Subsystem block, SIMULINK displays its underlying model. The figure below shows the result of opening the Subsystem block in the above model:

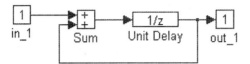

3.3.7 Modeling Equations

One of the most confusing issues for new SIMULINK users is how to model equations. Some examples will help you understand how to model them.

3.3.7.1 Converting Centigrade to Fahrenheit

Let's model the equation that converts Centigrade temperature to Fahrenheit:

$$T_F = 9/5(T_C) + 32$$

First, consider the blocks needed to build the model:

- A Gain block, to multiply the input signal by 9/5, from the Linear library
- A Constant block, to define a constant of 32, from the Sources library
- A Sum block, to add the two quantities, from the Linear library
- A Sine Wave block to input the signal, from the Sources library
- A Scope block to display the output, from the Sinks library

Next, gather the blocks into your model window:

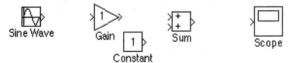

Assign values to the Gain and Constant blocks by opening (double-clicking on) each block and entering the appropriate values. Then, click on the **OK** button. Adjust the amplitude of the Sine Wave block to 10 to get more temperature variation.

Now, connect the blocks.

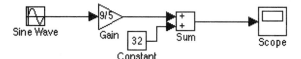

The Sine Wave represents Centigrade temperature. The Gain block generates $9/5(T_c)$. That value is added to the constant 32 by the Sum block. The output of that block is the Fahrenheit temperature. Open the Scope block to view the output. Set the horizontal scale to some short amount of time, say 10 seconds. Set the vertical scale so you can view all the output – at least 50. Keep the Scope block open.

Specify the simulation parameters by choosing **Parameters** on the **Simulation** menu. Specify a stop time of 10 seconds and a maximum step size of 0.1. Those values should run the simulation quickly. Now, choose **Start** on the **Simulation** menu to run the simulation.

3.3.7.2   Modeling a Simple Continuous System

Let's model the differential equation

$$\dot{x} = -2x + u$$

The Integrator block integrates its input, $\dfrac{dx}{dt}$, and produces x. Other blocks needed in this model include a Gain block and a Sum block. To generate a square wave, use a Signal Generator block. Again, view the output using a Scope block. Gather the blocks and define the Gain.

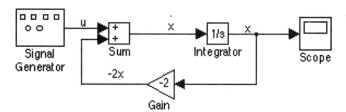

In this model, to reverse the direction of the Gain block, use the **Flip Horizontal** (on a Windows system) or **Flip** (on a Macintosh) command on the **Options** menu. Also, to create the line from the output of the Integrator block to the Gain block, hold down the **Ctrl** key (on a Windows system) or the **Option** key (on a Macintosh) while drawing the line. For more information, see "Drawing Lines from Other Lines" on page 42. Now you can connect all the blocks.

An important concept in this model is the loop that includes the Sum block, the Integrator block, and the Gain block. In this equation, x is the output of the

Integrator block as well as input to the blocks that compute $\dot{x}$, on which it is based. This relationship is implemented using a loop.

The Scope displays x at each time step. For a simulation lasting 10 seconds and Scope vertical range of 1, output looks like this:

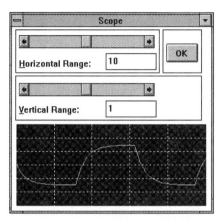

The equation you modeled in this example can also be expressed as a transfer function. The model uses the Transfer Fcn block, which accepts u as input and outputs x. So, the block implements x/u. If you substitute sx for $\dot{x}$ in the equation above, you get

$$sx = -2x + u$$

Solving for x gives us

$$x = u/(s+2)$$

Or,

$$x/u = 1/(s+2)$$

The Transfer Fcn block uses parameters to specify the numerator and denominator. In this case, the numerator is 1 and the denominator is s+2. Specify both terms as vectors of coefficients of successively decreasing powers of s; in this case the numerator is [1] and the denominator is [1 2].

The model now becomes quite simple:

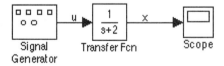

The results of this simulation are identical to those of the previous model.

3.4 Saving the Model

You can save a model by choosing either the **Save** or **Save As** command on the **File** menu. SIMULINK saves the model by generating an M-file that contains the MATLAB commands required to recreate the model.

If you are saving a model for the first time, use the **Save** command to assign a name and location to the M-file. Fill out the dialog box that appears and click on the **OK** button to save the file.

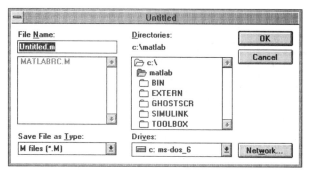

If you are saving a model whose M-file was previously saved, use the **Save** command to replace the M-file's contents or the **Save As** command to save the model with a new name or location. The **Save** command is destructive; that is, choosing this command will destroy the previous version of the model.

3.5 Printing a Block Diagram

You can print a block diagram by selecting **Print** on the **File** menu or by entering the `print` command in the MATLAB command window.

The **Print** command on the **File** menu prints the block diagram of the currently open system (or subsystem). This command does not print any open Scope blocks.

The MATLAB `print` command can direct its output to the printer or to a PostScript or Encapsulated PostScript (eps) file. This command does not print any open Scope blocks. The format of the `print` command is:

```
print -smodel -ddevice filename
```

where parameters are as follows:

model	The name of the system to be printed. If omitted, the current system is printed. The system must be open. If the system name contains spaces, use single quotes around the name. Represent newline characters as 13 (see the example below).
device	One of these PostScript or Windows devices:

PostScript devices include:

ps	PostScript for black and white printers
psc	PostScript for color printers
ps2	Level2 PostScript for black and white printers
psc2	Level2 PostScript for color printers
eps	Encapsulated PostScript (EPSF)
epsc	Encapsulated Color PostScript (EPSF)
eps2	Encapsulated Level 2 PostScript (EPSF)
epsc2	Encapsulated Level 2 Color PostScript (EPSF)

Windows devices include:

win	Currently installed printer, print in monochrome
winc	Currently installed printer, print in color
meta	Clipboard, in Metafile format
bitmap	Clipboard, in bitmap format
setup	Bring up **Print Setup** dialog box but do not print

filename	The PostScript file to which the output is saved. If filename exists, it is replaced. If filename does not include an extension, an appropriate one is appended.

When you specify one of the EPS device options (eps, epsc, eps2, and epsc2) but do not specify a filename, the print command automatically creates an EPS file. For example, the following command prints the current (untitled) model and automatically writes the output to an EPS file called Untitled.eps:

```
print —sUntitled —deps
```

MATLAB creates a file named after the model and issues this message:

```
Encapsulated PostScript files cannot be sent to printer.
File saved to disk under name 'Untitled.eps'.
```

If the system name contains spaces, the spaces are replaced with underscores.

For example, this command prints a system named Untitled:

```
print -sUntitled
```

The next command prints a system named Two-line System, a subsystem whose name appears on two lines. Output is written to a file named twoline.

```
print (['-sTwo-line' 13 'System'], 'twoline')
```

You cannot control the size of the system when print output is sent directly to the printer. If the diagram is larger than the page size, SIMULINK reduces it to fit the page. To control the size of the print output, direct output to an eps file or to a bitmap, then manipulate its size using a Word Processing program.

For more information about the `print` command, see the MATLAB documentation.

3.6 Tips for Building Models

Here are some hints that might help you be a more successful SIMULINK user.

- Memory issues

  In general, the more memory, the better SIMULINK performs. Less memory means that the simulation may not run to completion before needing to allocate more memory by swapping to disk, which slows down the simulation.

- Using hierarchy

  More complex models often benefit from adding the hierarchy of subsystems to the model. Grouping blocks simplifies the top level of the model and can make it easier to read and understand. For more information about grouping blocks into subsystems, see "Creating Subsystems" on page 46.

- Speeding up the simulation

  Slow simulation speed can have many causes. Here are a few:

  – MATLAB Fcn block – When a model includes a MATLAB Fcn block, the MATLAB interpreter is called at each time step. This drastically reduces simulation speed. Use the built-in Fcn block whenever possible.

  – Small step sizes or sample times (or mixing sample times that are not multiples of each other) – Keep the step size small enough to capture important events during the simulation. However, too small a step size may produce more output points than necessary and slow down the simulation. Step sizes are discussed in "Controlling the Step Size" in Chapter 4.

  – Algebraic loops – The solutions to algebraic loops are iterative and performed at every time step. Therefore, they severely degrade speed. For more information, see "Algebraic Loops" in Chapter 4.

  – Do not feed a Random Number block into an Integrator. For continuous systems use the Band-Limited White Noise block in the Sources library.

- Cleaning up models

  Clean and well organized models are easier to read and understand. Also, labels can help explain what is happening in a model. For more information, see "Adding Text Annotations to the Model Diagram" on page 46.

- Modeling strategies

  Generally, when building a model, work first on paper, then build it using the computer. When you start putting the blocks together using SIMULINK, add the blocks to the model window before adding the lines that connect them (this concept is called "collect, then connect"). This way, you can reduce the number of times you need to open block libraries.

Simulation and Analysis

This chapter discusses simulating models and analyzing the results. It discusses these topics:

- How SIMULINK works
- Simulation
- Linearization
- Equilibrium point determination

The "Simulation" section discusses how to specify simulation parameters and start a simulation, from the **Simulation** menu and from the MATLAB command window. It also discusses the different integration methods.

The analysis sections discuss the tools SIMULINK provides for linearization and equilibrium determination (trimming).

4.1 How SIMULINK Works

Each block within a SIMULINK model has these general characteristics: a set of inputs, u, a set of outputs, y, and a set of states, x:

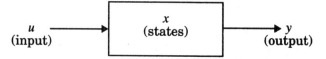

The state vector may consist of continuous states, discrete states, or a combination of both. The mathematical relationships between these quantities are expressed by these equations:

$$y = f_0(t, x, u) \qquad \text{(output)}$$

$$x_{d_{k+1}} = f_u(t, x, u) \qquad \text{(update)}$$

$$\dot{x}_c = f_d(t, x, u) \qquad \text{(derivative)}$$

$$\text{where} \quad x = \begin{bmatrix} x_c \\ x_{d_k} \end{bmatrix}$$

Simulation consists of two phases: initialization and simulation. Several actions take place during the initialization phase.

First, the block parameters are passed to MATLAB for evaluation. The resulting numerical values are used as the actual block parameters.

Next, the model hierarchy is flattened. Each subsystem is replaced by the blocks it contains.

Next, blocks are sorted into the order in which they need to be updated. The sorting algorithm constructs a list such that any block with direct feedthrough is not updated until the blocks driving its inputs are updated. It is during this step that algebraic loops are detected. For more information about algebraic loops, see the next section.

Finally, the connections between blocks are checked to ensure that the vector length of the output of each block is the same as the input expected by the blocks it drives.

Now the simulation is ready to run. A model is simulated using numerical integration. Each of the supplied integrators (simulation methods) depends on the ability of the model to provide the derivatives of its continuous states. Calculating these derivatives is a two-step process. First, each block's output is calculated in the order determined during the sorting. Then, in a second pass, each block calculates its derivatives based on the current time, its inputs, and its states. The resulting derivative vector is returned to the integrator, which uses it to calculate a new state vector. Once a new state vector is calculated, the sampled data blocks and scope blocks are updated.

4.1.1 Algebraic Loops

Algebraic, or implicit, loops occur when two or more blocks with direct feedthrough of their inputs form a feedback loop. When this occurs, SIMULINK must perform iterations at each step to determine whether there is a solution to this problem. Algebraic loops considerably reduce the speed of a simulation and may be unsolvable; avoid them whenever possible.

Examples of blocks with direct feedthrough are:

- Gain blocks
- Most nonlinear blocks (e.g., Look-Up Table, Rate Limiter)
- Transfer Fcn blocks, when the numerator and denominator are of the same order
- Zero-Pole blocks, when there are as many zeros as poles
- State-Space blocks, when there is a nonzero D matrix

This is a simple example of a system with an algebraic loop. The loop consists of the Sum, Transfer Fcn, and Gain blocks.

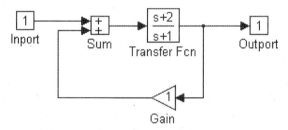

SIMULINK reports an error when it cannot solve an algebraic loop in 200 iterations of a Newton-Raphson routine.

To break algebraic loops, rather than allow SIMULINK to solve them iteratively, insert a Memory block between any two blocks included in the loop. The Memory block applies a one-integration-step delay. When used to break an algebraic loop, it is always the first block in the loop to be evaluated. You can also use a Transfer Fcn block or a Zero-Pole block. If a Transfer Fcn block is part of the loop, you can break the loop by adding a high-frequency pole of relatively small magnitude.

4.2 Simulation

You can run a simulation by selecting commands from the SIMULINK menus or by entering commands in the MATLAB command window.

- Selecting commands from the menus is quick to learn, simple to use, and can provide fast results. You can view the behavior of the system graphically with scopes. Working this way is most useful when you are creating and debugging a system.
- Entering simulation and analysis commands in the MATLAB command window or from scripts enables you to view the effects of changing block or

integration parameters. You can perform Monte-Carlo analysis by changing the parameters randomly and executing simulations in a loop.

Each of these methods may be appropriate at different stages of model development.

4.2.1 Simulation Parameters

Before you run a simulation, you should specify the simulation parameters and choose the integration method. The simulation parameters include:

- Start time and stop time
- Minimum and maximum integration step sizes
- Tolerance or relative error
- Return variables, if any

When you run the simulation using menu commands, you set the simulation parameters by selecting **Parameters** on the **Simulation** menu, then selecting an integration method and filling out the parameters in the **Control Panel** (Windows) or **Simulation parameters** (Macintosh) dialog box.

When you run the simulation using the command window, you specify parameters with the command that invokes the integration method and starts the simulation.

4.2.1.1 Start and Stop Time

The **Start Time** and **Stop Time** parameters specify the values of t at which the simulation is to start and end. Simulation time and wall clock time are not the same. For example, running a simulation for 10 seconds will usually not take 10 seconds. The amount of time it takes to run a simulation depends on many factors, including the model's complexity, the minimum and maximum step sizes, and the computer's clock speed.

4.2.1.2 Minimum Step Size

The **Minimum Step Size** parameter is the step size used at the start of a simulation. The integrators do not step below the minimum step size when generating an output point unless the system contains discrete blocks with sampling periods smaller than the minimum step size. An output point is a point generated in a sink, such as a Scope or To Workspace block, or returned in a state or output trajectory. An output point is generated after the minor iterations of the integration method have been completed.

Generally, the minimum step size should be set to a small value (e.g., 1e-6). However, when there are discontinuities in the system, setting the minimum step size to a very small value might cause an enormous number of points to be generated. This might overtax the memory and computing resources available. On the other hand, setting the minimum step size to a large value may result in an inaccurate simulation, as significant events may be missed.

For the adams and gear integration methods, the minimum step size does not affect the accuracy of the solution, but it does affect the number of output points generated. For these methods, it is best to set the minimum and maximum step sizes to values that produce output points that are good for plotting or analysis.

4.2.1.3 Maximum Step Size

Set the maximum step size small enough so that the simulation does not miss important details. A relatively large step size may cause some models to become unstable.

Sometimes a simulation produces results that are accurate but not good for producing smooth plots. In such a case, it may be necessary to limit the maximum step size so that a smooth plot results. For instance, it is often necessary to limit the step size in linsim when the system is linear and the inputs are piecewise linear, because this method is able to take arbitrarily large steps without losing accuracy. The rk45 method may also take large steps, which diminishes the quality of plotting.

4.2.1.4 Tolerance or Relative Error

The **Tolerance** (Windows) or **Relative Error** (Macintosh) parameter controls the acceptable relative error of the integration at each step of the integration. In general, this parameter should be set in the range 0.1 to 1e-6. The smaller the value, the more steps the integration takes, which results in a more accurate simulation. However, when the tolerance is set to a very small value (such as 1e-10), it may cause a step so small that roundoff error is significantly increased.

4.2.1.5 Return Variables

You can specify variable names in this field to cause SIMULINK to write values for the time, state, and output trajectories into the workspace. The first variable holds the time, the second holds the state, and the third holds the output.

4.2.2   Simulation from the Menu

Running a simulation from the menu allows you to perform **certain operations** interactively during a simulation:

- Change the parameters of a block, provided it does not **cause a change in the** number of states, inputs, or outputs for that block.
- Change any simulation parameter except return variables **and start time.**
- Change the simulation method.
- Simulate another system at the same time.
- Click on a line to see the signal carried on the line on **a floating (unconnected)** Scope block.

Changes to the structure of the model during a simulation, **such as adding or** deleting lines or blocks, cause the simulation to stop. Select **Start again to see** the result of the change.

Set the simulation parameters by choosing **Parameters** on the **Simulation** menu. SIMULINK displays the **Simulation parameters** (Macintosh) or **Control Panel** (Windows) dialog box, which appears below.

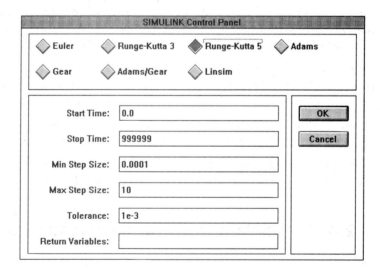

The **Simulation parameters** dialog box for the Macintosh appears below:

```
┌─────────────────────────────────────────────────────────────┐
│ Integration              Simulation parameters               │
│ algorithm                                          ╭────────╮ │
│   ○ Euler      Start Time        │0.0│             │   OK   │ │
│                                                    ╰────────╯ │
│   ○ RK-23      Stop Time         │999999│         ╭────────╮ │
│                                                   │ Cancel │  │
│   ◉ RK-45      Minimum Step Size │0.0001│         ╰────────╯ │
│   ○ Adams                                                     │
│   ○ Gear       Maximum Step Size │10│                        │
│                                                              │
│   ○ Adams/Gear Relative Error    │1e-3│                      │
│   ○ Linsim                                                   │
│                Return variables  │        │                  │
└─────────────────────────────────────────────────────────────┘
```

These dialog boxes enable you to choose the integration method **and define the simulation parameters**. You can specify parameters as numeric **values, vari-able** names, or valid MATLAB expressions. If you use variables, SIMULINK obtains values from the workspace. The integration methods **are described in** "Integration Methods" on page 65. The default method is the **Runge-Kutta-45** (fifth order).

When you have defined simulation parameters, you are **ready to run the simu-**lation. You run a simulation by selecting **Start** from the **Simulation menu. You** can also use the keyboard shortcut, **Ctrl-T** on a Windows system, or **⌘-T on a** Macintosh. When you start a simulation, the **Start** menu item **changes to Stop.**

If your model contains any Scope blocks, you must open them **to view the** output they display. SIMULINK automatically opens the graph **scopes: the** Auto-Scale Graph Scope, the Graph Scope, and the XY Graph **Scope blocks.**

To stop a simulation, choose **Stop** on the **Simulation** menu. The keyboard shortcut is **Ctrl-T** on a Windows system or **⌘-T** on a Macintosh.

You can suspend a running simulation by choosing **Pause** on the **Simulation** menu. Proceed with a suspended simulation by choosing **Continue.**

4.2.3   Simulation from the Command Line

Running a simulation from the command line has these **advantages over** running a simulation from the menu:

- You can override initial conditions for blocks (the x0 parameter).
- If you don't specify any left-hand arguments in the command **that starts the** simulation, MATLAB automatically plots the outputs or, if **there are no** outputs, the state trajectories.
- You can specify external inputs (using the ut parameter).

- You can run a simulation from an M-file, allowing parameters in the blocks to be iteratively changed.
- The simulation executes slightly faster.

The general format of the command that starts the simulation is:

```
[t,x,y] = method('model',tfinal,x0,options,ut)
```

Only the *method*, and the *model* and tfinal arguments are required. For detailed information on the command syntax, see "Integration Methods" in Chapter 7.

4.2.3.1   Specifying Initial Conditions of Blocks

Initial conditions, which are applied to the system at tstart, are generally set in the blocks themselves. You can override these initial conditions by providing an additional vector argument, x0. The initial conditions cannot be overridden if the model is simulated from the menu.

```
[t,x,y] = method('model',tfinal,x0);
```

When the x0 vector is empty ([ ]) or not specified, the initial conditions defined in the blocks are used.

You can determine a model's initial conditions with this command:

```
[sizes,x0] = model([], [], [], 0)
```

You can obtain the ordering of the states, which reflects how the block's initial conditions are ordered in the x0 vector, by adding a third left-hand argument:

```
[sizes,x0,xstr] = model([], [], [], 0)
```

where xstr is a string matrix whose i-th row contains the full path name of the block associated with the i-th state (and the i-th initial condition).

For example, this statement obtains the values of the initial conditions and the ordering of the states and initial conditions for the vdp model (the values for the sizes vector are omitted):

```
[sizes, x0, xstr] = vdp([], [], [], 0)

x0 =
    0.2500
    0.2500

xstr =
/vdp/int x2
/vdp/int x1
```

To show the block names for the Integrator blocks in the vdp model, select the Integrator blocks, then choose **Title** on the **Style** menu and select the **Displayed** option. To change the initial condition of the Integrator block labeled int x1, you enter

```
x0(2) = 0.50;
[t,x,y] = rk45('vdp', tfinal, x0);
```

This command uses the rk45 integration method.

4.2.3.1.1   Initial Conditions of Transfer Functions

The transfer function dialog boxes do not provide for the entry of initial conditions because there is no unique representation of transfer functions in terms of state variables. You can set initial conditions for these blocks by using the variable x0 in the call to the integration functions. In this case, the states represent those of a transfer function converted to state-space companion form as returned by the M-file tf2ss.

4.2.4   Viewing Output Trajectories

Output trajectories from SIMULINK can be plotted using one of three methods:

- Scope blocks
- Return variables and the MATLAB plotting commands
- To Workspace blocks and the MATLAB plotting commands

4.2.4.1   Using the Scope Block

The Scope block can be used to display output trajectories while the simulation is running. The simple model below shows an example of the use of the Scope block.

The display on the Scope is quite basic; it shows the output trajectory with no annotations. Graph scope blocks, such as the Auto-Scale Graph Scope block, the Graph Scope block, and the XY Graph Scope block, provide axis and colored line types but execute more slowly than the Scope block.

4.2.4.2   Using Return Variables

By returning time and output histories to MATLAB, you can use MATLAB's plotting commands to display and annotate the output trajectories.

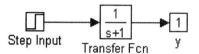

The block labeled y is an Outport block from the Connections library. The output trajectory, y, is returned by the integration function. For example, naming the system tfout and invoking the simulation from the command line:

```
[t,x,y] = linsim('tfout',2);
```

produces time histories. You could also run this simulation from the **Simulation** menu by specifying [t,x,y] as the **Return Variables** parameter. You can then plot these results using:

```
plot(t,y)
```

4.2.4.3   Using the To Workspace Block

The To Workspace block can be used to return output trajectories to the MATLAB workspace. The model below illustrates this:

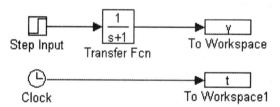

The variables y and t appear in the workspace when the simulation is complete. The time vector is stored by feeding a Clock block into a To Workspace block. The time vector can also be acquired by entering t in the **Return Variables** field for menu-driven simulations, or by returning it from the integration function:

```
t = linsim('tfout',2);
```

The To Workspace block can accept a vector input, with each input element's trajectory stored as a column vector in the resulting workspace variable.

4.2.5   Integration Methods

Simulation of SIMULINK models involves the numerical integration of sets of ordinary differential equations. SIMULINK provides a number of integration methods for the simulation of such equations:

`linsim`	Method that extracts the linear dynamics
`rk23`	Runge-Kutta third order method
`rk45`	Runge-Kutta fifth order method [1]
`gear`	Gear's predictor-corrector method for stiff systems [2]
`adams`	Adams' predictor-corrector method [2]
`euler`	Euler's method

A *stiff system* is one in which there are quickly and slowly changing dynamics and the quickly changing parts have reached steady state. Using a nonstiff method to solve a stiff system takes time steps on the time scale of the quickly changing part even though it's died away. A stiff method is capable of taking large time steps and ignoring the parts of the system whose behavior has reached steady state. [3]

4.2.5.1   Choosing a Method

Because of the diversity of dynamic system behavior, no single method simulates every type of model accurately and efficiently. Choosing the appropriate method and carefully selecting simulation parameters are important considerations for obtaining fast and accurate results.

Performance of the simulation in terms of speed and accuracy varies for different models and conditions. Use these guidelines when selecting a method.

4.2.5.1.1   linsim

`linsim` uses a method that extracts the linear dynamics of a system, leaving only the nonlinear dynamics of the system to be simulated. This method works very well when the system to be simulated is relatively linear. Linear models are composed of Transfer Fcn, State-Space, Zero-Pole, Sum, and Gain blocks. The method can take very large step sizes for such systems. Therefore, to obtain reasonably spaced output points, it is necessary to limit the maximum step size.

`linsim` is particularly good compared to other methods when the linear blocks have both fast and slow dynamics (i.e., stiff systems).

4.2.5.1.2   rk45, rk23

The Runge-Kutta methods, rk23 and rk45, are good general purpose methods that work well for a large range of problems [1]. These methods usually outperform the other methods when the system is highly nonlinear and/or discontinuous. These methods do not work well when the system has both fast and slow dynamics. In that case, use a stiff solver, such as linsim or gear. The rk23 and rk45 methods perform well for mixed continuous and discrete time systems.

Although rk45 is generally faster and more accurate than rk23, it produces fewer output points; therefore, rk23 may be the preferred choice for smoother plots.

4.2.5.1.3   adams, gear

adams and gear are predictor-corrector methods that work well on problems where the state trajectories are smooth [2]. Gear's method is designed for stiff systems. It is less efficient than other methods for nonstiff systems and does not work well when the system has discontinuities.

Use gear for systems that are smooth and nonlinear. It may not work well when there are singularities in the system or if the system is being perturbed by rapidly changing inputs.

Use adams for systems that are smooth and nonlinear but do not have widely varying time constants.

4.2.5.1.4   euler

euler is an implementation of the explicit forward Euler method, a first order method that will, in general, use more time points than higher order methods. This method does not produce results as accurate as other methods. You should avoid using it unless you are investigating execution of your model in real time.

4.2.5.2   Controlling the Step Size

The vector of integration parameters [tol,minstep,maxstep] in the command

```
[t,x,y] = linsim('model',tfinal,x0,[tol,minstep,maxstep]);
```

specifies tolerance, minimum step size, and maximum step size. The minstep and maxstep scalars can be used to limit the size of the integration step to minstep ≤ step size ≤ maxstep.

4.2.5.2.1   Fixed Step Methods

Although euler, linsim, rk23, and rk45 are variable step methods, they can be converted to fixed step methods by setting the minimum step size equal to the maximum step size:

```
[t,x,y] = linsim('model',tfinal,x0,[tol,fixstep,fixstep]);
```

The methods recognize when the minimum step size equals the maximum step size and avoid the error checking phase. Simulation is, therefore, more efficient but less accurate.

The adams and gear methods can take an undetermined number of points between outputs and, therefore, cannot be converted to fixed step methods. Specifying minimum and maximum step sizes with these methods ensures that SIMULINK captures data at points divisible by the step sizes.

4.2.5.2.2   Actual Step Size

At each time step, the integration methods call the model for its derivatives. This information is used to calculate the state derivatives and output. Each major step consists of a number of calls to the model for derivatives used to generate an output point. Only linsim and euler require one derivative call per output point. For other integration methods, it is possible that steps smaller than the minimum step size will be taken, because the integration step is subdivided. For rk45, six steps are taken for each output point generated in ratios in the following order: [0, 1/4, 3/8, 12/13, 1, 1/2]. For rk23, three steps are taken in the ratios [0, 1/2, 1]. The adams and gear functions use predictor-corrector methods, which take a variable number of steps between each output point.

The integrators may take steps back in time when the error exceeds the tolerance parameter. This generally happens when there are nonlinearities in the system.

4.2.5.3   Interpolating Data

The integration methods automatically vary the step size to produce output points that are within local error estimates. This means that the integration may produce unevenly spaced points, which makes it difficult to compare the results from different simulation runs. Using MATLAB interpolation functions, you can interpolate data to estimate points at the appropriate times.

In this example, a system is used to generate an approximation for the average error of a low tolerance simulation; you can compare this result to a high tolerance simulation by linearly interpolating the data using MATLAB's interp1 function:

```
% High tolerance simulation
[t,x,y] = linsim('system',10,[],[1e-8,1e-6,1]);
% Low tolerance simulation
[tl,xl,yl] = linsim('system',10,[],[0.1,1e-5,1]);
% Linearly interpolate
```

```
[yint] = interp1(t,y,tl);
err_per_point = sum(abs(yint - yl))/length(tl);
```

Polynomial interpolation methods are more suitable when you need to generate more data points than are available from the simulation. For example, to perform bilinear interpolation to increase the number of points for a smoother plot, use MATLAB's `interp2` function:

```
% Generate 200 points for plotting
tfine = 0:.05:10;
[t,x,y] = rk45('system',10,[],[1e-2,1e-4,1]);
% Interpolate over finer time scale
yint = interp2(t,y,tfine)
plot(tfine,yint)
```

Similarly, cubic spline interpolation is performed using MATLAB's `spline` command. This method is not recommended for large data sets because of its memory requirements.

```
yint = spline(t,y,tfine)
```

4.2.5.4   Comparing the Methods: An Example

Simulation performance depends on the choice of methods and parameter settings. This example compares the simulation methods by using the Van der Pol equation, a simple second order nonlinear model:

$$\ddot{x} + (x^2 - 1)\dot{x} + x = 0$$

This equation can be described as a set of first order differential equations:

$$\dot{x}_1 = x_1(1 - x_2^2) - x_2$$
$$\dot{x}_2 = x_1$$

These equations are represented as the vdp system, provided with SIMULINK.

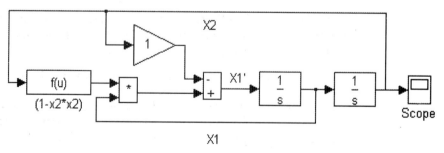

In this example, we compare the integration methods using a tolerance parameter value of 1e-3. The integration parameters are defined as:

```
tol = 1e-3;
minstep = 1e-5;
maxstep = 10;
options = [tol,minstep,maxstep];
x0 = [1;1];
```

We compare the integration methods linsim, rk23, and **rk45**:

```
[tls,xls] = linsim('vdp',10,x0,options);
[tr23,xr23] = rk23('vdp',10,x0,options);
[tr45,xr45] = rk45('vdp',10,x0,options);
plot(tls,xls,tr23,xr23,'o',tr45,xr45,'+')
```

The plot of the three state trajectories is:

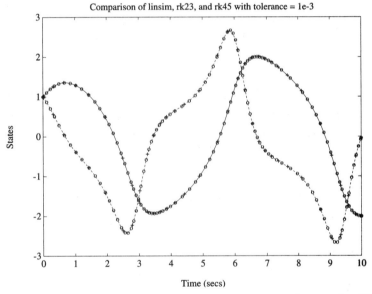

This plot shows that there is good agreement among the results. **If you compare** the adams and gear methods, you will find those results consistent **with the** results obtained using the other methods.

This table compares the methods at a tolerance of 1e-3:

Method	Derivative Calls	Output Points	Execution Time (Ratio)	Error Per Point
linsim	144	136	1.37	0.0061
rk23	316	89	1.60	0.0023
rk45	204	35	1	0.0041

Method	Derivative Calls	Output Points	Execution Time (Ratio)	Error Per Point
adams	270	55	1.51	0.0019
gear	336	65	1.91	0.0049
euler	365	366	3.03	0.2881

The euler method results are included in the table, although they are not shown graphically because of the substantial error.

Let's compare the simulation results using an error tolerance of 0.1:

```
options(1) = 0.1;
```

Again, we compare the integration methods linsim, rk23, and rk45. To save the time entering these commands, use the up arrow key to access previous MATLAB commands.

```
[tls,xls] = linsim('vdp',10,x0,options);
[tr23,xr23] = rk23('vdp',10,x0,options);
[tr45,xr45] = rk45('vdp',10,x0,options);
```

This time, a graph is plotted against a trajectory obtained using rk45 with a tolerance of 1e-6:

```
[t,x] = rk45('vdp',10,x0,[1e-6,1e-5,10]);
plot(t,x,tls,xls,'x',tr23,xr23,'—',tr45,xr45,':')
```

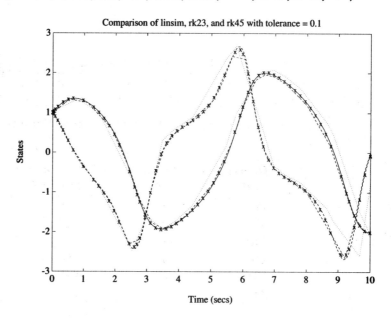

Comparison of linsim, rk23, and rk45 with tolerance = 0.1

Some degradation is noticeable in the responses. The response generated with linsim shows the best fit. The rk45 responses (dotted line) show considerable degradation.

We compare the adams, gear, and euler methods with a tolerance of 0.1:

```
[ta,xa] = adams('vdp',10,x0,options);
[tg,xg] = gear('vdp',10,x0,options);
[te,xe] = euler('vdp',10,x0,options);
plot(t,x,ta,xa,'x',tg,xg,'—',te,xe,':')
```

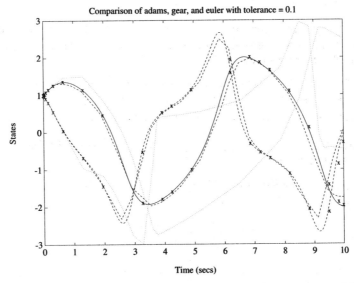

Notice that the euler method (dotted line) has become unstable. The adams and gear methods show some deviation from the desired response.

The number of derivative calls for the methods at a tolerance of 0.1 are shown in this table:

Method	Derivative Calls	Output Points	Execution Time (Ratio)	Error Per Point
linsim	77	74	2.38	0.0326
rk23	86	23	1.29	0.3730
rk45	140	21	1.46	0.8811
adams	116	34	2.69	0.1005
gear	181	48	4.17	0.2319
euler	33	34	1	1.5835

It is important to note that these statistics are for the simulation of one system only. They are not a valid representation of the overall performance of the integration methods, although they do demonstrate how the methods perform differently and how the simulation parameters can affect the results in different ways.

4.2.6 Discrete-Time Systems

SIMULINK has the ability to simulate discrete (sampled data) systems. Models can be *multirate*; that is, they can contain blocks that are sampled at different rates. Models can be constructed solely from discrete blocks, or they can be hybrid, containing a mixture of discrete and continuous blocks.

4.2.6.1 Discrete Blocks

Each of the discrete blocks has a built-in sampler at its input and a zero-order hold at its output. When the discrete blocks are mixed with continuous blocks, the output of the discrete blocks between sample times is held constant. The inputs to the discrete blocks are updated only at times that correspond to sample hits.

4.2.6.2 Sample Time

The **Sample time** parameter sets the sample time at which a discrete block's states are updated. Normally, the sample time is set to a scalar variable; however, it is possible to specify an offset time (or skew) by specifying a two-element vector in this field.

For example, specifying the **Sample time** parameter as the vector [Ts,offset] sets the sample time to Ts and the offset value to offset. The discrete block is updated on integer multiples of the sample time and offset values only:

```
t = n * Ts + offset
```

where n is an integer and offset can be positive or negative, but not greater than the sample time. The offset is useful if some discrete blocks must be updated sooner or later than others.

You cannot change the sample time of a block while a simulation is running. If you want to change a block's sample time, you must stop and restart the simulation for the change to take effect.

4.2.6.3 Purely Discrete Systems

Purely discrete systems can be simulated using any of the integration methods; there is no difference in the solutions. To achieve output points that reflect sample hits only, set the minimum step size to a value greater than the maximum sample time.

4.2.6.4 Multirate Systems

Multirate systems contain blocks that are sampled at different rates. These systems can be modeled with discrete blocks or both discrete and continuous blocks. For example, consider this simple multirate discrete model:

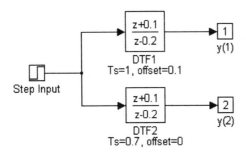

The Step Input block's **Step time** parameter is changed from 1 to 0. The **Sample time** and **Offset** parameters of the DTF1 Discrete Transfer Fcn block are set to 1 and 0.1, respectively; the **Sample time** of the DTF2 Transfer Fcn block is set to 0.7 with no offset. Invoking the simulation and plotting the outputs using the stairs function:

```
[t,x,y] = euler('multirate',3);
stairs(t,y)
```

produces this plot:

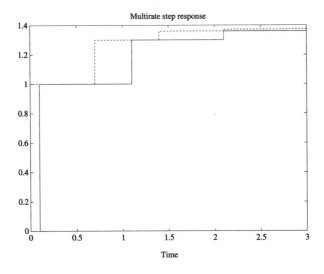

In this example, the output from y(1) is the solid line, and the output from y(2) is the dotted line. For the DTF1 block, which has an offset of 0.1, there is no feedthrough of the inputs until t=0.1. Since the initial conditions of the transfer functions are zero, the output of DTF1 is zero before this time. If the output of DTF1 must be 1 at t=0, set the offset to –0.9.

4.2.6.5   Sample Time Colors

The sample time colors feature helps you easily identify different sample rates in your model. This feature shows sample rates by applying the color scheme shown in the table below.

To understand how this function works, it is important to be familiar with SIMULINK's Sample Time Propagation Engine (STPE). The figure below illustrates a discrete Filter block with a sample time of Ts driving a Gain block. Because the Gain block's output is simply the input multiplied by a constant, its output changes at the same rate as the filter. In other words, the Gain block has an effective sample rate equal to that of the filter's sample rate. This is the fundamental mechanism behind the STPE.

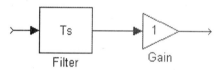

To enable the sample time colors feature, select **Sample Time Colors** in the **Style** menu.

SIMULINK does not automatically recolor the model with each change you make to it, so you must select **Update Diagram** on the **Style** menu whenever you want to update the model coloration. To return to your original coloring, disable sample time coloration by again choosing **Sample Time Colors**.

4.2.6.5.1   What the Colors Mean

When using sample time colors, the color assigned to each block depends on its sample time with respect to other sample times in the model. This table describes how the colors are used:

Color	Assigned To
Black	Continuous blocks
Yellow	Hybrid (subsystems grouping blocks with varying sample times or muxes/demuxes grouping signals with varying sample times)
Red	Fastest discrete sample time
Green	Second fastest discrete sample time

Color	Assigned To
Blue	Third fastest discrete sample time
Cyan	Fourth fastest discrete sample time

Sample times for individual blocks are set according to the following rules:

- Continuous blocks (e.g., Integrator, Derivative, Transfer Fcn, etc.) are, by definition, continuous.

- Discrete blocks (e.g., Zero-Order Hold, Unit Delay, Discrete Transfer Fcn, etc.) have sample times that are explicitly specified by the user on the respective dialog boxes.

- All other blocks have implicitly defined sample times that are based on the sample times of their inputs. For instance, a Gain block that follows an integrator is treated as a continuous block, whereas a Gain block that follows a Zero-Order Hold is treated as a discrete block having the same sample time as the Zero-Order Hold that is driving it.

  For multi-input blocks with inputs having disparate sample times, the block is assigned the sample time of the fastest input if all of the other sample times are integer multiples of it; otherwise the block is considered to be continuous.

If the model has more than four sample rates, the four fastest rates are colored red, green, blue, and cyan. Additional rates are colored yellow and SIMULINK issues an appropriate message.

It is important to note that Mux and Demux blocks are simply grouping operators – signals passing through them retain their timing information. For this reason, the lines emanating from a Demux block may have unique colors if they are driven by sources having different sample times. In this case the Mux and Demux blocks are color coded as hybrids (yellow) to indicate that they handle signals with multiple rates.

Similarly, subsystem blocks that contain blocks with differing sample times are also colored as hybrids, since there is no single rate associated with them. If all of the blocks within a subsystem run at a single rate, then the subsystem block is colored according to that rate.

Under some circumstances, SIMULINK also backpropagates sample times to source blocks if it can do so without affecting the output of a simulation. For instance, in the model below, SIMULINK recognizes that the Signal Generator is driving a Discrete-Time Integrator so it assigns the Signal Generator and the Gain block the same sample time as the Discrete-Time Integrator block.

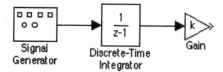

You can verify this by enabling **Sample Time Colors** and noting that all blocks are colored red. Because the Discrete-Time Integrator block only looks at its input at its sample times, this change does not affect the outcome of the simulation but does result in a performance improvement.

Replacing the Discrete-Time Integrator block with a continuous Integrator block, as shown below, and recoloring the model by choosing **Update Diagram** on the **Style** menu cause the Signal Generator and Gain blocks to change to continuous blocks, as indicated by their being colored black.

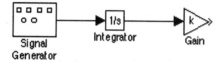

4.2.6.6 Mixed Continuous and Discrete Systems

Mixed continuous and discrete systems are composed of both sampled and continuous blocks. Such systems can be simulated using any of the integration methods, although certain methods can be more efficient and accurate than others. For most mixed continuous and discrete systems, the Runge-Kutta variable step methods, rk23 and rk45, are superior to the other methods in terms of efficiency and accuracy. Due to discontinuities associated with the sample and hold of the discrete blocks, the gear and adams methods are not recommended for mixed continuous and discrete systems.

4.3 Linearization

SIMULINK provides the functions `linmod` and `dlinmod` to extract **linear models** in the form of the state-space matrices *A*, *B*, *C*, and *D*. State-space matrices describe the linear input-output relationship as

$$\dot{x} = Ax + Bu$$
$$y = Cx + Du$$

where x, u, and y are state, input, and output vectors, respectively. For example, the following model is called `lmod`.

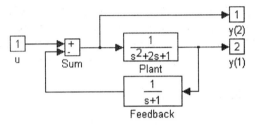

To extract the linear model of this SIMULINK model, enter this command to get the linear model that follows:

```
[A,B,C,D] = linmod('lmod')
A =
        -1      0      1
        -1     -2     -1
         0      1      0
 B =
         0
         1
         0
 C =
         0      0      1
        -1      0      0
 D =
         0
         1
```

Inputs and outputs must be defined using Inport and Outport blocks from the Connections library. The Signal Generator and Scope blocks do not act as inputs and outputs. Inputs can be used in conjunction with Signal Generator blocks using a Sum block. Once the data is in the state-space form, you can apply functions in the Signals and Systems Toolbox in the Student Edition of MATLAB for further analysis:

- Conversion to transfer function form:

```
[num,den] = ss2tf(A,B,C,D);
```

- Bode phase and magnitude frequency plot:

```
bode(A,B,C,D)
```

- Linearized time response:

```
step(A,B,C,D)
impulse(A,B,C,D)
lsim(A,B,C,D,u,t)
```

Other functions can be used for linear control system design.

When the model is nonlinear, an operating point must be chosen at which to extract the linearized model. The nonlinear model is also sensitive to the perturbation sizes at which the model is extracted. These must be selected to balance the trade-off between truncation and round-off error. Extra arguments to linmod specify the operating point and perturbation points:

```
[A,B,C,D] = linmod('model', x, u, pert, xpert, upert)
```

For discrete systems or mixed continuous and discrete systems, use the function dlinmod for linearization. This has the same calling syntax as linmod except that the second right-hand argument must contain a sample time at which to perform the linearization. For more information, see the description of the linmod command in Chapter 7.

Using linmod to linearize a model that contains Derivative or Transport Delay blocks can be troublesome. Before linearizing, replace these blocks with specially designed blocks that avoid the problems. These blocks are in the Extras library in the Alternative Blocks for Linearization sublibrary.

- For the Derivative block, use the Switched derivative for linearization block.
- For the Transport Delay block, use the Switched transport delay for linearization block.

When using a Derivative block, you can also try to incorporate the derivative term in other blocks. For example, if you have a Derivative block in series with a Transfer Fcn block, it is better implemented (although this is not always possible) with a single Transfer Fcn block of the form

$$\frac{s}{s + a}$$

4.4 Equilibrium Point Determination (trim)

The SIMULINK function trim determines steady-state equilibrium points. Consider, for example, the model called lmod:

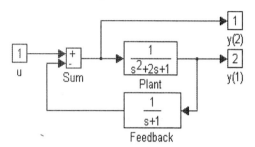

For example, you can use the trim function to find the values of the input and the states that set the outputs to 1. First, we make initial guesses for the state variables (x) and input values (u), then set the desired value for the output (y):

```
x = [0; 0; 0];
u = 0;
y = [1; 1];
```

Use index variables to indicate which variables are fixed and which can vary:

```
ix = [];    % Don't fix any of the states
iu = [];    % Don't fix the input
iy = [1;2]; % Fix both output 1 and output 2
```

Invoking trim returns the solution. Your results may differ due to round-off error.

```
[x,u,y,dx] = trim('lmod',x,u,y,ix,iu,iy)

x =

     1.0000
     0.0000
     1.0000
u =

     2
y =

     1.0000
     1.0000
```

```
dx =
    1.0e-15 *
    0
    0.4441
    0.2693
```

Note that there may be no solution to equilibrium point problems. If that is the case, `trim` returns a solution that minimizes the maximum deviation from the desired result after first trying to set the derivatives to zero. The `trim` syntax description is included in Chapter 7.

4.5 References

[1] Forsythe, G. F., M.A. Malcolm, C.B. Moler, *Computer Methods for Mathematical Computations*, Prentice Hall, 1977.

[2] Kahaner, D., C.B. Moler, S. Nash, *Numerical Methods and Software*, Prentice Hall, 1989.

[3] Shampine, L. F., *Numerical Solution of Ordinary Differential Equations*, Chapman & Hall, 1994.

5

Using Masks to Customize Blocks

Using SIMULINK's masking function, you can customize blocks or subsystems by creating a new dialog box and, optionally, a new block icon. This chapter discusses these topics:

- Overview of the Masking Process
- Creating a Masked Block
- Defining Icons for Masked Blocks

5.1 Overview of the Masking Process

Masking provides these benefits:

- Shields your model users from unnecessary complexity
- Provides a descriptive and helpful user interface
- Protects the contents of blocks from unintended tampering

An important use of masking is that it allows you to create a single dialog box to accept parameters for more than one block in a subsystem. As a result, instead of having to provide parameter values for several blocks on many dialog boxes, you can combine those blocks into a subsystem and define a single dialog box to accept values for those parameters.

Creating a mask for this use involves these steps:

1. Open each block, assigning variable names for the parameters whose values you want to provide in the new dialog box.

2. Create the subsystem. For more information, see "Creating Subsystems" in Chapter 3.

3. Select the subsystem block, then choose **Mask** on the **Options** menu.

4. Fill in the masking dialog box. The next section discusses this step in detail.

5. Click the **OK** button to create the masked block. The subsystem block displays the icon you defined on the masking dialog box. If you open the masked subsystem block, SIMULINK displays the new dialog box you created.

5.2   Creating a Masked Block

Suppose we want to create a simple second order system block and define a new block icon and dialog box. Masking the Transfer Fcn block allows us to define its parameters, the natural frequency (wn) and the damping coefficient (zeta), as variables instead of having to specify the numerator and denominator each time we run the simulation.

Let's build a simple model using a Sine Wave block as input, a Transfer Fcn block, and a Scope block. In the Transfer Fcn block's dialog box, define the numerator as [wn^2] and the denominator as [1 2*zeta*wn wn^2]. When we connect the blocks, the model looks like this:

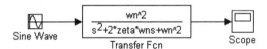

Sine Wave   Transfer Fcn   Scope

5.2.1   Filling Out the Mask Dialog Box

To mask the Transfer Fcn block, select the block, then choose **Mask** from the **Options** menu. The masking dialog box, which appears below, lets you describe the masked block by defining its parameter fields, initialization commands, icon, and help text. The dialog box title and the block name and type are derived from the block being masked, in this example, Transfer Fcn.

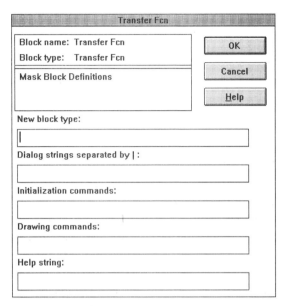

SIMULINK creates a new dialog box and icon for the masked block using the information you provide on this dialog box: the block type, its title, its dialog box parameter field labels, how the block is initialized, what the block's icon looks like, and the text displayed when you press the **Help** button on the block's dialog box.

The figure below shows the dialog box we create in this exercise and how the parts of that dialog box are related to the parameter fields on the dialog box used to create the mask:

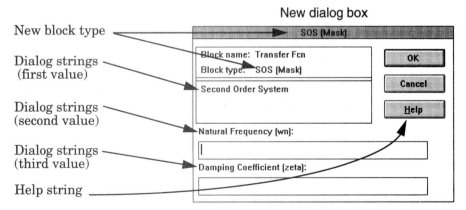

New dialog box

The sections below discuss each parameter field on the masking dialog box.

5.2.1.1 The New Block Type Field

Specify the block type for the masked block in the **New block type** field. The block type is an arbitrary block description that has no effect on the block's performance. It appears in the block's dialog box as the title and as the text in the **Block type** field. For this example, enter:

```
SOS
```

SIMULINK adds "(Mask)" after the text.

5.2.1.2 The Dialog Strings Field

The **Dialog strings** field defines these parts of the new dialog box:

• The block description

• The parameter field labels

You specify these values using the following format:

```
BlockDesc|Parameter₁Label|Parameter₂Label|...|ParameterₙLabel
```

Separate values with a vertical bar (|). It is not necessary to enter spaces before and after the vertical bars. To force a line break in the block description, add \n characters.

You can define up to six parameter fields. If you need to define more than six parameters, you must define one or more fields to accept vectors that hold more than one parameter. For example, you can combine the **Natural Frequency** and **Damping Coefficient** fields into a single field, then enter values for them as a vector. The field, with values entered, might look like this (the vertical bar after the closing bracket is the cursor):

Natural Frequency (wn) and Damping Coefficient (zeta):

```
[2.0, 0.707]
```

If this were the first parameter field defined for the dialog box, you would reference the Natural Frequency value (2.0) with this initializing command:

```
wn = @1(1);
```

and reference the Damping Coefficient value (0.707) with this command:

```
zeta = @1(2);
```

For more information about how SIMULINK references block parameter values in initialization commands, see "The Initialization Commands Field" on page 85.

5.2.1.2.1   Specifying the Block Description

The block description appears as informative text in the box under the block name and type. For this example, enter:

```
Second Order System
```

5.2.1.2.2   Specifying Parameter Fields and Labels

You create parameter fields for the new dialog box by entering their labels after the block description. For this example, the masked block's dialog box provides fields for the natural frequency and damping coefficient. Enter the following (the text includes the block description, which you already entered):

```
Second Order System|Natural Frequency (wn):|Damping Coefficient (zeta):
```

5.2.1.2.3   Specifying a *MATLAB* Command

If you want SIMULINK to evaluate a MATLAB command instead of opening the block's dialog box, you specify that command in this field. To specify a MATLAB command, include it in an `eval` statement (see your MATLAB documentation for details) and do not specify the block description and parameter field labels.

For example, entering the following command in the **Dialog strings** field plots a straight line graph every time the block is double-clicked:

```
eval('plot(1:10)')
```

5.2.1.3   The Initialization Commands Field

Specify how the block is initialized in the **Initialization commands** field. Initialization commands can use values entered in the parameter fields in the new mask dialog box. When you define the initialization commands, you reference these user-entered values by their relative *position* on the dialog box of the new mask using this format:

```
variable=@field
```

`variable` is the name of the variable as it is specified in the underlying (masked) block's dialog box. `field` is a number that indicates the parameter field on the new mask dialog box. @1 references the user input in the first parameter field, @2 references the second parameter field, etc.

For this example, the natural frequency is determined by the value entered in the **Natural Frequency** parameter field, the first parameter field in the new dialog box. The variable name (wn) is the same name used in the **Transfer Fcn** block dialog box. Specify the initialization command for the natural frequency as:

```
wn=@1;
```

Similarly, the damping coefficient is the value entered in the **Damping Coeffi-cient** (the second) parameter field. Specify both initialization commands as follows:

```
wn=@1; zeta=@2;
```

5.2.1.3.1   Scope of Initialization Variables

Variables you specify in the **Initialization commands** field are local to this dialog box. They are available to other initialization commands on this dialog box and to any of the underlying blocks. Also, initialization commands cannot access variables in the workspace, although underlying blocks can.

For example, if we define an initialization command as wn=x*@1; where x is a workspace variable, SIMULINK will signal an error. Also, wn is only accessible by the masked dialog box or an underlying block's dialog box (the Transfer Fcn block in this example) and is not written to the workspace.

5.2.1.3.2   Echoing Initialization Command Results

Specifying an assignment statement without a terminating semicolon echoes its results to the command window. Leaving off the semicolons can be useful for debugging, when it is helpful to see what values are being assigned to the block parameters.

5.2.1.4   The Drawing Commands Field

You can define a new block icon by specifying a command in the **Drawing commands** field. You can enter text, a plot command, or transfer function parameters. If you enter a long text string, use \n to indicate a line break. It is not necessary to enter spaces before or after the \n.

For this example, specify a text label:

```
Second Order\nSystem
```

For information about creating other kinds of icons, see "Creating Icons for Masked Blocks" on page 89.

5.2.1.5   The Help String Field

You can optionally specify a help entry for the masked block in the **Help string** field. The text you enter gets displayed when you click on the **Help** button on the masked block's dialog box.

To include line breaks in the help text, include \n where you want the line to break. It is not necessary to include spaces before or after the \n. For this example, you can leave this field blank.

5.2.2 Creating the Masked Block Icon and Dialog Box

When you've entered values in these fields, click on the **OK** button. SIMULINK creates the icon and dialog box, with field labels, initialization commands, and the help string as you defined them. The icon and dialog box for this masked block appear below.

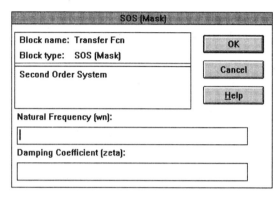

When you enter values for these fields and click on the **OK** button, the initialization commands assign those values to the natural frequency (wn) and damping coefficient (zeta) variables used in the masked Transfer Fcn block.

5.2.3 Creating Default Values for Masked Block Parameters

As the dialog box above shows, the **Natural Frequency** and **Damping Coefficient** parameter fields are empty when the masked block's dialog box appears. If you want to assign default values (or "factory settings") for parameters that show up each time you open the block, you need to save the default values with the block. To do this, enter the values and click on the **OK** button. Then, when you save the model, these values will be saved along with the block.

5.2.4 Masking Subsystems That Contain Masked Blocks

You can create complex, multilevel masks in SIMULINK, passing variables through many masking layers. To create these masks, simply mask the subsystem that contains the masked block or blocks, using the same variable names in each layer. SIMULINK passes those parameters to the appropriate block when the user enters values on the masked block's dialog box

5.2.5   Unmasking a Masked Block

You can unmask a masked block by selecting the block, then choosing **Unmask** from the **Options** menu. SIMULINK displays the block (or subsystem) with its default icon.

Important. To retain masking information about a block you unmask, you must mask that block before you unmask another block. Otherwise, the masking information is lost.

The figure below illustrates the relationship between the original unmasked block and the new masked block.

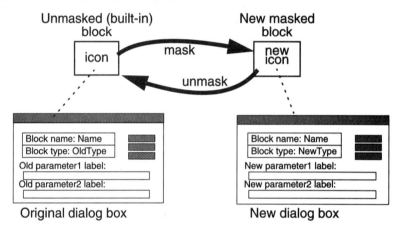

5.2.6   Modifying Masking Information for a Block

To modify masking information for a block, follow these steps:

1. Select the block.

2. Choose **Mask** on the **Options** menu. The current mask dialog box appears.

3. Modify the information and click on the **OK** button.

5.3 Creating Icons for Masked Blocks

You can provide a more distinctive or descriptive icon for your masked block by specifying information in the **Drawing commands** field on the Mask dialog box. Using this field, you can create icons that show descriptive text, state equations, or graphics.

5.3.1 Displaying Text in the Icon

To display text in the block icon, enter the text in the **Drawing commands** field. To insert a line break in the icon label, enter \n. It is not necessary to add a space before or after the \n. For example, the figure below shows two samples of text entered in the **Drawing commands** field and the resulting icons.

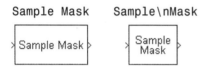

5.3.2 Displaying Transfer Functions in the Icon

To display a continuous transfer function in the block icon, enter the following command in the **Drawing commands** field:

```
dpoly(num, den)
```

For the example used earlier in this chapter, you could specify

```
dpoly([wn^2],[1 2*zeta*wn wn^2])
```

When you create the mask, the block icon displays the transfer function. When you run the model and enter values for the **Natural Frequency** and **Damping Coefficient** parameters, SIMULINK evaluates the transfer function and displays the resulting equation in the icon. For example, if you enter 2 and 0.707 for the parameters, the block icon would appear like this:

$$\frac{4}{s^2+2.83s+4}$$

To display a discrete transfer function in descending powers of z, enter:

```
dpoly(num, den, 'z')
```

To display a discrete transfer function in ascending powers of *1/z*, enter:

```
dpoly(num, den, 'z-')
```

To display a zero pole gain transfer function, enter this command:

```
droots(z, p, k)
```

When you enter any of these commands and click on the **OK** button, SIMULINK displays error messages indicating that a parameter is undefined. SIMULINK is unable to generate the transfer function equation until values are entered for the parameters in the masked block's dialog box. Until then, the block icon displays three questions marks. When the user enters values, the icon changes to reflect the drawing command results.

5.3.3   Displaying Graphics in the Icon

You can display a plot on your masked block icon by entering the `plot` command in the **Drawing commands** field. This `plot` command is similar to the MATLAB `plot` command except that you do not specify line types and you must specify vectors in x,y pairs, unless the data is complex. There is no limit to the number of x,y pairs and the plot is auto-scaled.

For example, the following command displays the plot on the Pulse Generator block icon, in the Sources library:

```
plot(0,0,100,100,[90,75,75,60,60,35,35,20,20,10],
[20,20,80,80,20,20,80,80,20,20])
```

To examine drawing commands used to generate plots on SIMULINK masked blocks, follow this procedure:

1. Copy the block into your model window.

2. Select the block, then choose **Mask** on the **Options** menu. SIMULINK displays the Mask dialog box. Examine the **Drawing commands** field.

3. To retain the block as a masked block, click on the **OK** button.

If the plot is dependent on variables defined in the mask, the block icon will display three question marks until values are entered for those variables.

5.3.4 Using iconedit to Create the Icon

The `iconedit` utility provides an easy way to generate simple graphics for an icon. To use `iconedit`, type `iconedit` in the MATLAB command window. MATLAB asks you to identify the model window and the block whose icon you want to create, then displays a figure window with an axis and grid lines.

To begin drawing graphics, follow these simple steps:

1. Position the cross-hairs cursor where you want the plot to start and click on the mouse button. An asterisk appears on the grid at the cursor location. If you click the mouse button in the wrong place, type d to delete that point.

2. Move the cursor where you want the next point to appear and click on the mouse button. `iconedit` connects the lines and draws another asterisk at the second point.

3. Continue moving the cursor and clicking the mouse button. Type q when you finish. `iconedit` displays the command that generates the plot in the command window, enters the command in the **Display commands** field of the block's mask dialog box, and generates the icon.

6

Block Reference

This chapter provides reference information for all SIMULINK blocks. Blocks appear in alphabetical order and contain this information:

- The block name and icon.

- The purpose of the block.

- The block library that contains the block.

- A description of the block's use.

- The block's dialog box and parameters (if any). Parameters can be entered as valid MATLAB expressions. Variables used in those expressions must exist in the workspace.

- The block's characteristics, including some or all of these:

  - Scalar expansion – whether or not scalar values are expanded to vectors. Some blocks expand scalar inputs or parameters as appropriate. For more information, see "Scalar Expansion of Inputs and Parameters" in Chapter 3.

  - Sample Time – how the block's sample time is determined, whether by the block itself (as is the case with discrete and continuous blocks) or inherited from the block that drives it.

  - States – how many discrete and continuous states.

  - Direct Feedthrough – whether the block has direct feedthrough. For more information, see "Algebraic Loops" in Chapter 4.

The SIMULINK Block Libraries

SIMULINK organizes its blocks into block libraries according to their behavior. The **simulink** window, shown "SIMULINK Windows and Menus" in Chapter 3, displays the icons and library names.

The *Sources* library includes blocks that originate signals. The table below describes the blocks in the Sources library.

Block Name	Purpose
Band-Limited White Noise	Introduce white noise into continuous systems.
Chirp Signal	Generate sine wave with increasing frequency.
Clock	Display and provide simulation time.
Constant	Generate a constant value.
Digital Clock	Generate simulation time at specified sampling interval.
From File	Read data from a file.
From Workspace	Read data from a matrix defined in the workspace.
Pulse Generator	Generate pulses at regular intervals.
Random Number	Generate normally distributed random numbers.
Repeating Sequence	Generate a regularly repeatable arbitrary signal.
Signal Generator	Generate various waveforms.
Sine Wave	Generate a sine wave.
Step Input	Generate a step function.

The *Sinks* library includes blocks that display or write block output. The table below describes the blocks in the Sinks library.

Block Name	Purpose
Auto-Scale Graph Scope	Display signals in auto-scaled MATLAB figure window.
Graph Scope	Display signals in MATLAB figure window.
Hit Crossing	Increase the number of simulation steps around a specified value.
Scope	Display signals during simulation.
Stop Simulation	Stop simulation when input is nonzero.
To File	Write data to a file.
To Workspace	Write data to a matrix in the workspace.
XY Graph Scope	Display X-Y plot of signals in MATLAB figure window.

The *Discrete* library contains blocks that describe discrete-time components. The table below describes the blocks in the Discrete library.

Block Name	Purpose
Discrete-Time Integrator	Perform discrete-time integration of a signal.
Discrete-Time Limited Integrator	Perform discrete-time integration of a signal with limits.
Discrete State-Space	Implement a discrete state-space system.
Discrete Transfer Fcn	Implement a discrete transfer function.
Discrete Zero-Pole	Implement a discrete transfer function in terms of poles and zeros.
Filter	Implement IIR and FIR filters.
First-Order Hold	Implement a first order sample-and-hold latch.
Unit Delay	Delay a signal one sample period.
Zero-Order Hold	Implement zero-order hold of one sample period.

The *Linear* library contains blocks that describe standard linear functions. The table below describes the blocks in the Linear library.

Block Name	Purpose
Derivative	Output the time derivative of the input.
Gain	Multiply block input.
Inner Product	Generate dot product.
Integrator	Integrate a signal.
Matrix Gain	Multiply input by a matrix.
Slider Gain	Vary a scalar gain using a slider.
State-Space	Implement a linear state-space system.
Sum	Generate the sum of inputs.
Transfer Fcn	Implement a linear transfer function.
Zero-Pole	Implement a transfer function specified in terms of poles and zeros.

The *Nonlinear* library contains blocks that describe standard nonlinear functions. The table below describes the blocks in the Nonlinear library.

Block Name	Purpose
Abs	Output the absolute value of the input.
Backlash	Model the behavior of a system with play.
Combinatorial Logic	Implement a truth table.
Coulombic Friction	Model discontinuity at zero with linear gain elsewhere.
Dead Zone	Provide a region of zero output.

Block Name	Purpose
Fcn	Apply a specified expression to the input.
Limited Integrator	Integrate within specified levels.
Logical Operator	Perform specified logical operation on the input.
Look-Up Table	Perform piecewise linear mapping of the input.
MATLAB Fcn	Apply a MATLAB function to the input.
Memory	Output the block input at the previous integration step.
Product	Multiply inputs together
Quantizer	Discretize input at a specified interval.
Rate Limiter	Limit the rate of change of a signal.
Relational Operator	Perform specified relational operation on the input.
Relay	Switch output between two values.
Reset Integrator	Reset integrator states during simulation.
Saturation	Limit excursion of a signal.
Sign	Return the sign of the input.
Switch	Switch between two inputs.
Transport Delay	Delay the input by a given amount of time.
2-D Look-Up Table	Perform piecewise linear mapping of two inputs.
Variable Transport Delay	Delay the input by a variable amount of time.

The *Connections* library contains blocks that allow multiplexing and demultiplexing, implement external Input/Output, and create subsystems. The table below describes the blocks in the Connections library.

Block Name	Purpose
Demux	Separate vector signal into output signals.
Inport	Provide a link to an external input and for linearization.
Mux	Combine several input lines into a vector line.
Outport	Provide a link to an external output and for linearization.
Subsystem	Represent a system within another system.

The *Extras* library contains demo programs and several sublibraries: the Conversions library, the Flip-Flops library, the PID Controllers library, the Analyzers library, the Filter library, and a sublibrary of blocks to be used with linearization. These libraries are described in Appendix B.

Abs

Output the absolute value of the input   *Nonlinear library*

Description

The Abs block generates as output the absolute value of the input. The block accepts one input and generates one output; both can be scalar or vector.

Dialog Box

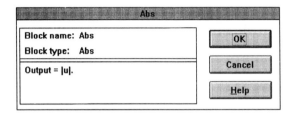

Characteristics

Sample Time	Inherited from driving block
States	0
Direct Feedthrough	Yes

Auto-Scale Graph Scope

Display signals using auto-scaled MATLAB figure window   *Sinks library*

Description

The Auto-Scale Graph Scope block plots its input in a MATLAB figure window, automatically scaling the graph limits to keep the data on the graph.

The block accepts one input, which can be scalar or vector. The block plots the input with respect to simulation time. Initially, the plotting area is defined by the **Initial Time Range** parameter in the x direction and the **Initial y-min** and **Initial y-max** parameters in the y direction. After the simulation starts, the y values are automatically scaled to the minimum and maximum values of the signal.

The block stores the input and time data in a buffer, whose size is specified by the **Storage points** parameter. This parameter value is the maximum number of points the block can display before shifting the origin.

If the input is a vector, the scope plots each signal according to colors, line types, and plot symbols specified by the **Line type** parameter.

For a demo that illustrates the use of the Auto-Scale Graph Scope block, enter lorenz2 in the command window.

Parameters and Dialog Box

Initial Time Range
The initial x-axis. The default is five seconds.

Initial y-min
The initial lower limit for the y-axis. The default is -10.

Initial y-max
The initial upper limit for the y-axis. The default is 10.

Storage points
The maximum number of points that can be displayed on the scope. The default is 200 points.

Line type
The color and line type or plot symbol for the output, enclosed in single quotation marks. Separate line types with a slash (/). For information about these codes, see the plot command in the *Student Edition of MATLAB User's Guide*. The default is 'y-/g--/c-./w:/m*/ro/b+'.

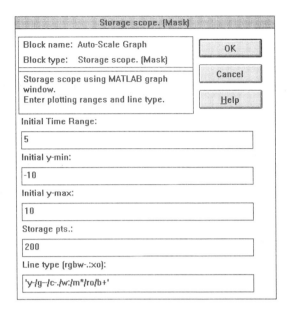

Characteristics   Sample Time   Inherited from driving block
                        States   9 discrete (used internally)

Backlash

Model the behavior of a system with play   *Nonlinear library*

Description

The Backlash block implements a system in which a change in input causes an equal change in output except within an area of specified width, in which no change in output occurs. This area is called the *deadband*.

This block can be thought of as a relay with infinite output levels. Its behavior is like that of a system whose input is a shaft with a gear on the end of it and whose output is another shaft with a gear on the end driven by the input shaft. If the teeth of the gears are spaced far enough apart, the system has *play*.

The block accepts one input and generates one output. Both can be scalar or vector.

At the start of the simulation, the position of the output is specified by the **Initial output value** parameter and the width of the deadband is specified by the **Deadband width** parameter. The initial input value is at the center of the deadband. The block's output is determined by these conditions:

• While the input is within the deadband, the output remains constant.

• When the input reaches either end of the deadband, a change in input in that direction results in an equal change in the output.

The figures below illustrates the block's operation. The first figure shows the relationship between the input, the output, and the block parameters:

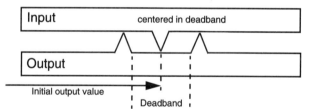

The Initial State of the Backlash Block

The next figure shows the state of the block when the input has reached the end of the deadband and "engaged" the output.

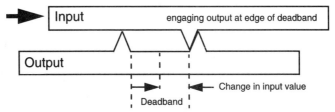

The State when Input and Output Are Engaged

The final figure shows how a change in input affects the output while they are engaged.

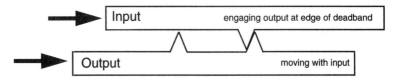

ΔOutput = ΔInput While Engaged

If the top shaft (the input) reverses its direction, its teeth disengage from the bottom shaft (the output). The output remains constant until the input reaches the opposite end of the deadband. Now, as before, movement in the input is reflected by equal movement in the output.

For example, the following model and the plot that follows it show the effect of a sine wave passing through a Backlash block.

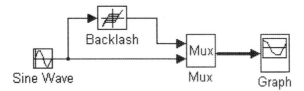

The deadband is 1 and the initial output value is 0. Notice in the plot below that the output (the solid line) is zero until the input reaches the end of the deadband (at 0.5). Now, the input and output are engaged and the output moves as the input does until the input changes direction (at 1.0). When the input reaches 0, it again engages the output at the opposite end of the deadband.

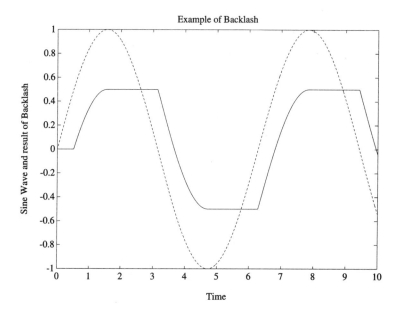

Parameters and Dialog Box

Deadband width
The width of the deadband.

Initial input value
The difference between the **Initial input value** and the **Initial output value** must not exceed the width of the deadband.

Initial output value
The initial output value.

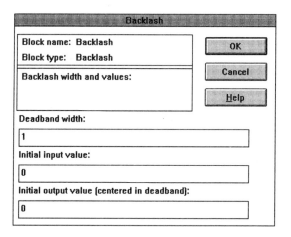

Characteristics

Scalar Expansion	Of parameters
Sample Time	Inherited from driving block
States	0
Direct Feedthrough	Yes

Band-Limited White Noise

Introduce white noise into continuous systems   *Sources library*

Description

The Band-Limited White Noise block generates samples of white noise for input to continuous systems. The block generates one output, which can be scalar or vector.

This block produces an approximation of continuous white noise. The block is implemented by passing white noise through a Zero-Order Hold block. It increases the signal amplitude to compensate for the loss in signal bandwidth (and energy) that occurs as you increase the sample time.

Parameters and Dialog Box

Noise Power

The **Noise Power** and **Seed** parameters can be vectors of the same length to produce a vector of white noise signals. The default value is [0.1].

Sample Time

To make the simulation execute faster, set the sample time to the highest value possible but consistent with the fastest dynamics of the system. Sample time must be a scalar. The default value is 0.1.

Seed

Used to generate the white noise. The **Noise Power** and **Seed** parameters can be vectors of the same length to produce a vector of white noise signals. The default value is [23341].

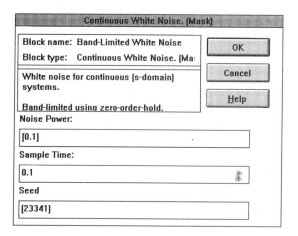

Characteristics   Sample Time   Discrete
                       States   0

Chirp Signal

Generate sine wave with increasing frequency   *Sources library*

Description

The Chirp Signal block generates a sine wave whose frequency increases at a linear rate with time. You can use this block for spectral analysis of nonlinear systems. The block generates one scalar output.

Parameters and Dialog Box

Initial frequency (Hz)
The initial frequency of the signal. The default is 0.1 Hz.

Target time (secs)
The time at which the frequency reaches the **Frequency at target time** parameter value. The frequency continues to change at the same rate after this time. The default is 100 seconds.

Frequency at target time
The frequency of the signal at the target time. The default is 1 Hz.

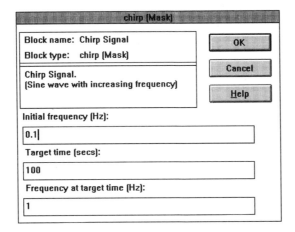

Characteristics

Sample Time	Continuous
States	0

Clock

Display and provide the simulation time   *Sources library*

Description   The Clock block outputs the current simulation time at each major simula-
tion step. When the block is opened, this time is displayed in the window.
Running a simulation with this block open slows down the simulation. The
Clock block is useful for other blocks that need the simulation time.

Dialog Box

Characteristics   Sample Time   Continuous
                       States   0

Combinatorial Logic

Implement a truth table   *Nonlinear library*

Description
The Combinatorial Logic block implements a standard truth table for modeling programmable logic arrays (PLAs), logic circuits, decision tables, and other Boolean expressions. You can use this block in conjunction with Memory blocks to implement finite-state machines or flip-flops.

You enter a matrix of possible outputs as the **Truth table** parameter. Each column of the matrix corresponds to a different output and each row contains the output for a different combination of inputs. The number of rows is 2^n where n is the number of inputs. It is not necessary to enter the input combinations. You must specify outputs for every combination of inputs. The output can consist of any combination of numerical values; it is not constrained to the values of one and zero.

The block accepts one vectorized input that determines which output value is selected from the truth table. The truth table rows follow the conventional order where the first row is [0 0 0...0] (all inputs are 0) and the last row is [1 1 1...1] (all inputs are 1). The number of digits depends on the number of inputs. Any nonzero input value is treated as a 1.

The first output value is referenced by an input vector of [0 0 ... 0 0], the second by a vector of [0 0 ... 0 1], the third by [0 0 ... 1 0], and so on.

The Combinatorial Logic block has one input port and one output port.

Example - A two-input AND function

For example, the outputs for a two-input AND function are specified as:

```
[0; 0; 0; 1]
```

which corresponds to this truth table:

Input 1	Input 2	Output
0	0	0
0	1	0
1	0	0
1	1	1

If the input vector is [1, 0], the input references the third row. So, the output value is 0.

Example - A binary adder

This circuit has three inputs: the two bits (a and b) to be summed, and a carry-in bit (c). It has two outputs, the sum bit (s) and the carry-out bit (c').

The truth table for this circuit is

a	b	c	c'	s
0	0	0	0	0
0	0	1	0	1
0	1	0	0	1
0	1	1	1	0
1	0	0	0	1
1	0	1	1	0
1	1	0	1	0
1	1	1	1	1

To implement this adder with the Combinatorial Logic block, you would enter the 8-by-2 matrix formed by columns c' and s as the **Truth table** parameter. There is no need to specify the inputs; these are implicitly included in the block in the order that they are displayed in the table.

Note that sequential circuits, i.e., circuits with states, can also be implemented with the Combinatorial Logic block by including an additional input for the state of the block and feeding the output of the block back into this state input.

Parameters and Dialog Box

Truth table

The matrix of outputs. Each column corresponds to an output and each row corresponds to a row of the truth table.

```
┌─────────────── Combinatorial Logic ───────────────┐
│                                                    │
│  Block name:  Combinatorial Logic    ┌────────┐   │
│                                      │   OK   │   │
│  Block type:   Combinatorial Logic    └────────┘   │
│  ────────────────────────────────    ┌────────┐   │
│  Non-zero inputs index the rows      │ Cancel │   │
│  of the truth table which are        └────────┘   │
│  given as outputs.                   ┌────────┐   │
│                                      │  Help  │   │
│  ────────────────────────────────    └────────┘   │
│  Truth table:                                      │
│  ┌──────────────────────────────────────────────┐ │
│  │ [0 0;0 1;0 1;0 0 1;1 0;1 0;1 1]              │ │
│  └──────────────────────────────────────────────┘ │
└────────────────────────────────────────────────────┘
```

Characteristics

Input Vector Width	$\log_2$ of the length of the logic table
Output Vector Width	Number of columns of the logic table

Sample Time	Inherited from driving block
States	0
Direct Feedthrough	Yes

Constant

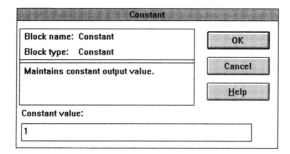

Generate a constant value   *Sources library*

Description   The Constant block generates a specified value independent of time. The
                      block generates one output, which can be scalar or vector, depending on the
                      size of the **Constant value** parameter. The block displays the specified value
                      on its icon.

Parameters and   **Constant value**
Dialog Box   The output of the block. If a vector is specified, the output is a vector of
                      constants. The default value is 1.

Characteristics   Sample Time   Constant
                      States   0

Coulombic Friction

Discontinuity at zero, with linear gain elsewhere   *Nonlinear library*

Description   The Coulombic Friction block has a discontinuity at zero and a linear gain
afterwards. It is implemented as:

```
y = sign(u) * (Gain * abs(u) + Offset)
```

where y is the output, u is the input, and `Gain` and `Offset` are block parameters.

The block accepts one input and generates one output; both can be scalar
or vector.

Parameters and   **Offset discontinuity at zero**
Dialog Box   The amount of the offset, applied to all input values.

Gain
The signal gain at nonzero input points.

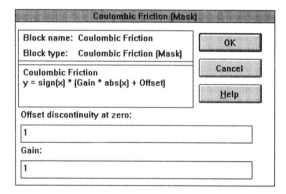

Characteristics   Scalar Expansion   No
Sample Time   Inherited from driving block
States   0
Direct Feedthrough   Yes

Dead Zone

Provide a region of zero output   *Nonlinear library*

Description   The Dead Zone block generates zero output within a specified region, called its dead zone. The lower and upper limits of the dead zone are specified as the **Start of dead zone** and **End of dead zone** parameters. The block generates output according to the input and dead zone:

- If the input is greater than the lower limit and less than the upper limit, the output is zero.

- If the input is greater than the upper limit, the output is the upper limit minus the input.

- If the input is less than the lower limit, the output is the input less the lower limit.

- If the lower and upper limits are equal, the output is the value of the input minus the dead zone value.

The block accepts one input and generates one output; both can be scalar or vector.

The following is a sample model using lower and upper limits of -.5 and +.5, with a sine wave as input.

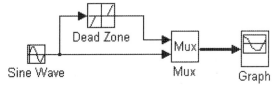

The following plot shows the effect of the Dead Zone block on the sine wave:

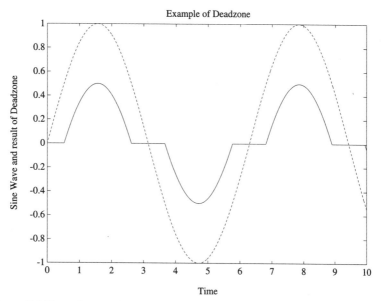

The solid line shows the output of Dead Zone block.

Parameters and Dialog Box

Start of dead zone
The lower limit of the dead zone.

End of dead zone
The upper limit of the dead zone.

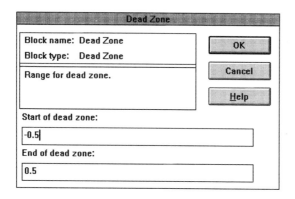

Characteristics

Scalar Expansion	Of parameters
Sample Time	Inherited from driving block
States	0
Direct Feedthrough	Yes

Demux

Separate a vector signal into output signals   *Connections library*

Description

The Demux block separates a vector line into several output lines.

The input to a Demux block is a vector of any width. The block generates a specifiable number of outputs, which can be scalars and/or vectors.

SIMULINK draws the Demux block output ports to reflect the specified number of outputs, resizing the block if necessary.

Parameters and Dialog Box

Number of outputs

The number and width of outputs. The total of the output widths must match the width of the input line. Specify a vector of -1 values to indicate that the output is dynamically sized; this is described in more detail below.

For scalar outputs, specify the number of outputs or -1. The block produces one output for each input vector element. The m-th output is the m-th input vector element.

For outputs of equal width, specify the number of outputs. For example, if the input vector has 12 elements and you want to generate three 4-element output vectors, specify 3.

For vector outputs of unequal width (including one or more scalar outputs), you can specify the number and size of the outputs or you can specify the number of outputs and have the block determine their sizes.

- Specify the number and size of the outputs explicitly by entering them as a vector. For example, [4 1 2] generates three outputs from a 7-element input vector: the first output is the first four elements, the second output is the fifth element, and the third output is the sixth and seventh elements.

- Specify the number of the outputs and let the block determine one or more of their sizes. You can do this in these ways:

  Specify the number of outputs as a scalar. The block determines their widths by dividing the input width by the number of outputs. If the outputs are not equal sizes, the block makes them as close in size as possible. For example, if the input vector has nine elements and you specify two outputs, the first output has five elements and the second has four. If outputs do not have the same size, SIMULINK displays a warning.

  Specify a vector as a combination of scalars and -1 values. The block allocates the number of elements for the outputs whose sizes are specified as scalars, then divides the remaining elements across the outputs specified as -1. If the elements do not divide evenly, SIMULINK displays a warning in the command window.

For example, if you specify [4 −1 −1] and the input vector has eight elements, the first output has four elements and the second and third outputs have two elements each, dividing the remaining four elements evenly. If, instead, you specify [5 −1 −1], the first output has five elements and the remaining three elements are divided unevenly, with the second output having two elements and the third output having one element. SIMULINK issues a warning message in both instances.

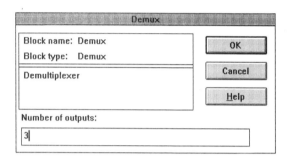

Characteristics

Scalar Expansion	N/A
Sample Time	Inherited from driving block
States	0
Direct Feedthrough	Yes

Derivative

Output the time derivative of the input   *Linear library*

Description   The Derivative block approximates the derivative of its input by computing

$$\frac{\Delta u}{\Delta t}$$

where Δu is the change in input value and Δt is the change in time since the previous major simulation time step. The block accepts one input and generates one output, both of which can be scalar or vector. The initial input for the block is zero.

The accuracy of the results depends on the size of the time steps taken in the simulation. Smaller steps allow a smoother and more accurate output curve from this block. Unlike other blocks that have continuous states, the integration algorithm will not take smaller steps when the input changes rapidly.

Using linmod to linearize a model that contains a Derivative block can be troublesome. For information about how to avoid the problem, see "Linearization" in Chapter 4.

Dialog Box

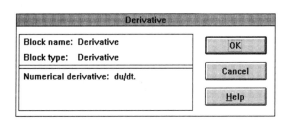

Characteristics

Scalar Expansion	N/A
Sample Time	Continuous
States	0
Direct Feedthrough	Yes

Digital Clock

Generate simulation time at specified sampling interval　　　　　　　*Sources library*

Description　　　The Digital Clock block outputs the current simulation time only at the specified sampling interval. At other times, the output is held at the previous value.

Use this block rather than the Clock block (which outputs continuous time) when you need the current time within a discrete system. Using this block improves the efficiency of code generated for multirate systems with the professional SIMULINK Real-Time Workshop.

Parameters and Dialog Box　　**Sample time**

The sampling interval. The default value is one second.

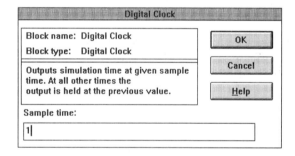

Characteristics　　Sample Time　　　　　　　　Discrete

　　　　　　　　　　　States　　　　　　　　　　　　0

Discrete State-Space

$$x(n+1)=Ax(n)+Bu(n)$$
$$y(n)=Cx(n)+Du(n)$$

Implement a discrete state-space system   *Discrete library*

Description   The Discrete State-Space block implements the system described by

$$x(n+1) = Ax(n) + Bu(n)$$
$$y(n) = Cx(n) + Du(n)$$

where u is the input, x is the state, and y is the output.

The block accepts one input and generates one output, both of which can be scalar or vector. The input vector width is determined by the width of the B and D matrices. The output vector width is determined by the width of the C and D matrices.

The sample time can be specified with an optional offset; see the description of the **Sample time** parameter below.

Parameters and   **A, B, C, D**
Dialog Box   The matrix coefficients as defined in the above equations.

• A must be an n-by-n matrix, where n is the number of states.

• B must be an n-by-m matrix, where m is the number of inputs.

• C must be a q-by-n matrix, where q is the number of outputs.

• D must be a q-by-m matrix.

Initial conditions
The initial state vector. If not supplied, it is assumed to be zero.

Sample time
The time interval between samples. The sample time is specified as a scalar or a two-element vector. The first element is the sample time; the second element, if present, is the offset time. The offset time allows the sample hit to be offset from the end of the sample period. A positive offset specifies a lag; a negative offset specifies a lead for each sample hit.

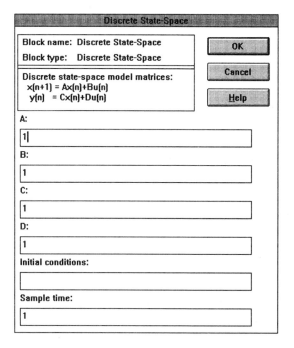

Characteristics

Sample Time	Discrete
States	Variable, determined by the size of A
Direct Feedthrough	Only if $D \neq 0$

Discrete-Time Integrator

$$\boxed{\dfrac{1}{z\text{-}1}}$$

Perform discrete-time integration of a signal   *Discrete library*

Description   The Discrete-Time Integrator block implements a vectorized version of a
discrete Euler integration scheme equivalent to the following z-domain
transfer function:

$$y = \frac{T_s}{z-1} \cdot u$$

where y is the output, T_s is the sample time, and u is the input.

This block can be used in place of the continuous integrator (1/s) block
when constructing a purely discrete system. The block accepts one input
and generates one output, both of which can be scalar or vector.

Parameters and   **Initial Condition**
Dialog Box   The initial condition, which can be specified as a constant or a variable. If
the block input is a vector and the initial value is specified as a vector, they
must be the same size. If the initial value is specified as a scalar, scalar
expansion takes place. The m-th element of the input vector is integrated
with the initial value specified by the m-th element of the initial value
vector to produce the m-th element in the output vector.

Sample Time
The time interval between samples. The sample time is specified as a
scalar or a two-element vector. The first element is the sample time; the
second element, if present, is the offset time. The offset time allows the
sample hit to be offset from the end of the sample period. A positive offset
specifies a lag; a negative offset specifies a lead for each sample hit.

Discrete-Time Integrator (Mask)	
Block name: Discrete-Time Integrator	OK
Block type: Discrete-Time Integrator (M	
Discrete-Time Integrator:	Cancel
	Help
Initial Condition:	
0		
Sample Time:	
1	

Characteristics

Scalar Expansion	Of **Initial Condition** parameter
Sample Time	Discrete
States	Variable
Direct Feedthrough	No

Discrete-Time Limited Integrator

Perform discrete-time integration of a signal with limits   *Discrete library*

Description   The Discrete-Time Limited Integrator block prevents the output of a
Discrete-Time Integrator block from exceeding specified levels.

This block accepts one input and generates one output, both of which can
be scalar or vector.

Parameters and   **Lower bound**
Dialog Box   The lower limit of the block output.

Upper bound
The upper limit of the block output.

Initial condition
The initial condition, which can be specified as a constant or a variable. If
the block input is a vector and the initial value is specified as a vector, they
must be the same size. If the initial value is specified as a scalar, scalar
expansion takes place. The m-th element of the input vector is integrated
with the initial value specified by the m-th element of the initial value
vector to produce the m-th element in the output vector.

Sampling Time
The time interval between samples. The sample time is specified as a
scalar or a two-element vector. The first element is the sample time; the
second element, if present, is the offset time. The offset time allows the
sample hit to be offset from the end of the sample period. A positive offset
specifies a lag; a negative offset specifies a lead for each sample hit.

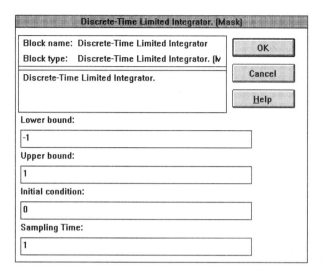

Characteristics

Scalar Expansion	Of bounds and **Initial condition** parameters
Sample Time	Discrete
States	Inherited from driving block or parameters
Direct Feedthrough	No

Discrete Transfer Fcn

Implement a discrete transfer function
Discrete library

Description
The Discrete Transfer Fcn block implements the *z*-transform transfer function described by the following equations:

$$H(z) = \frac{num(z)}{den(z)} = \frac{num(1)\,z^{nn-1} + num(2)\,z^{nn-2} + \ldots + num(nn)}{den(1)\,z^{nd-1} + den(2)\,z^{nd-2} + \ldots + den(nd)}$$

where *nn* and *nd* are the number of numerator and denominator coefficients, respectively. Row vectors *num* and *den*, specified as parameters, contain the coefficients of the numerator and denominator, respectively, in descending powers of *z*. A vector of *n* elements specifies a polynomial of degree *n–1*. The order of the denominator must be greater than or equal to the order of the numerator. The block accepts one scalar input and generates one scalar output.

The Discrete Transfer Fcn block represents the method typically used by control engineers, representing systems as polynomials in *z* or *s*. The Filter block represents the method typically used by signal processing engineers, who describe systems using polynomials in z^{-1} (the delay operator). The two are identical when the numerator is the same length as the denominator.

The Discrete Transfer Fcn block displays the numerator and denominator within its icon depending on how they are specified. See the description of the Transfer Fcn block on page 191 for more information.

Parameters and Dialog Box

Numerator
The vector of numerator coefficients. The default is [1].

Denominator
The vector of denominator coefficients. The default is [1 0.5].

Sample time
The time interval between samples. The sample time is specified as a scalar or a two-element vector. The first element is the sample time; the second element, if present, is the offset time. The offset time allows the sample hit to be offset from the end of the sample period. A positive offset specifies a lag; a negative offset specifies a lead for each sample hit.

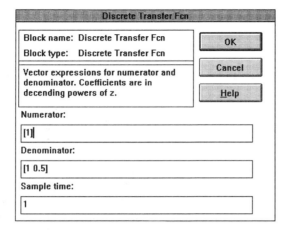

Characteristics

Scalar Expansion	N/A
Sample Time	Discrete
States	Length of **Denominator** parameter -1
Direct Feedthrough	Yes, if the lengths of the **Numerator** and **Denominator** parameters are equal

Discrete Zero-Pole

$$\frac{(z\text{-}1)}{z(z\text{-}0.5)}$$

Implement a discrete transfer function in terms of poles and zeros   *Discrete library*

Description   The Discrete Zero-Pole block implements a discrete system with the speci-fied zeros, poles, and gain in terms of the delay operator z. The block accepts one scalar input and generates one scalar output.

A transfer function can be expressed in factored or zero-pole-gain form, which, for a single-input single-output system in MATLAB, is:

$$H(z) = K\frac{Z(z)}{P(z)} = K\frac{(z-Z(1))\,(z-Z(2))\dots(z-Z(n))}{(z-P(1))\,(z-P(2))\dots(z-P(n))}$$

where Z represents the zeros vector, P represents the poles vector, and K represents the scalar gain.

The Discrete Zero-Pole block displays the transfer function in its icon depending on how the parameters are specified. See the description of the Zero-Pole block on page 203 for more information.

Parameters and   **Zeros**
Dialog Box   The vector of zeros. The default is [1].

Poles
The vector of poles. The default is [0; 0.5].

Gain
The gain, entered as a number or variable. The default is [1].

Sample time
The time interval between samples. The sample time is specified as a scalar or a two-element vector. The first element is the sample time; the second element, if present, is the offset time. The offset time allows the sample hit to be offset from the end of the sample period. A positive offset specifies a lag; a negative offset specifies a lead for each sample hit.

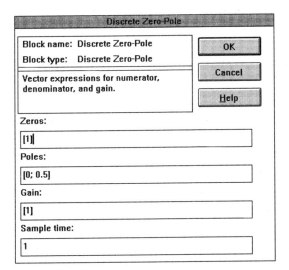

Characteristics

Scalar Expansion	No
Sample Time	Discrete
States	Length of **Poles** vector
Direct Feedthrough	Yes, if the numbers of poles and zeros are equal

Fcn

> sin(u[1])

Apply a specified expression to the input

Nonlinear library

Description

The Fcn block applies the specified C language style expression to its input. The expression can be made up of one or more of these components:

- u — the input to the block. If u is a vector, u[i] represents the i-th element of the vector; u[1] or u alone represents the first element. Note that square brackets are used to index into the input vector.

- Numeric constants

- Arithmetic operators (+ − * /)

- Relational operators (== != > < >= <=) — The expression returns 1 if the relation is TRUE; otherwise, it returns 0.

- Logical operators (&& || !) — The expression returns 1 if the relation is TRUE; otherwise, it returns 0.

- Parentheses

- MATLAB functions — abs, acos, asin, atan, atan2, ceil, cos, cosh, exp, fabs, floor, hypot, ln, log, log10, pow, power, rem, sgn, sin, sinh, sqrt, tan, tanh

- Workspace variables — Variable names that are not recognized in the list of items above are passed to MATLAB for evaluation. Matrix or vector elements must be specifically referenced (e.g., A(1,1) instead of A for the first element in the matrix).

Block input can be a scalar or vector. The output is always a scalar.

Parameters and Dialog Box

Expression

The C language style expression applied to the input. Expression components are listed above. The expression must be mathematically well formed (i.e., matched parentheses, proper numbers of function arguments, etc.). The expression differs from a MATLAB expression in these ways:

- The expression cannot perform matrix computations.

- The expression references elements of the input, u, using square brackets, although references to workspace variables use parentheses.

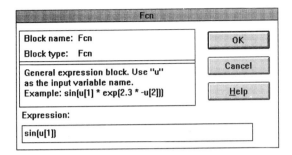

Characteristics

Scalar Expansion	No
Sample Time	Inherited from driving block
States	0
Direct Feedthrough	Yes

Filter

$$\frac{1}{1+2z^{-1}}$$

Implement IIR and FIR filters   *Discrete library*

Description   The Filter block implements the Infinite Impulse Response (IIR) and Finite Impulse Response (FIR) filters. The block accepts one scalar input and generates one scalar output.

You specify the coefficients of the numerator and denominator polynomials in ascending powers of z^{-1} as vectors using the **Numerator** and **Denominator** parameters. The order of the denominator must be greater than or equal to the order of the numerator. See the Discrete Transfer Fcn block description on page 124 for more information about coefficients.

The Filter block represents the method typically used by signal processing engineers, who describe systems using polynomials in z^{-1} (the delay operator). The Discrete Transfer Fcn block represents the method typically used by control engineers, representing the system as polynomials in z or s. The two are identical when the numerator is the same length as the denominator. A vector of n elements specifies a polynomial of degree $n-1$.

The Filter block displays the numerator and denominator in its icon depending on how they are specified. For a discussion of how SIMULINK displays the icon, see the Transfer Fcn block description on page 191.

Parameters and Dialog Box   **Numerator**
The vector of numerator coefficients. The default is [1].

Denominator
The vector of denominator coefficients. The default is [1 2].

Sample time
The time interval between samples. The sample time is specified as a scalar or a two-element vector. The first element is the sample time; the second element, if present, is the offset time. The offset time allows the sample hit to be offset from the end of the sample period. A positive offset specifies a lag; a negative offset specifies a lead for each sample hit.

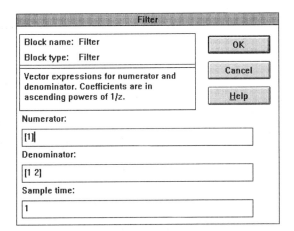

Characteristics

Scalar Expansion	N/A
Sample Time	Discrete
States	Length of **Denominator** parameter - 1
Direct Feedthrough	Yes, if the lengths of the **Numerator** and **Denominator** parameters are equal

First-Order Hold

Implement a first-order sample-and-hold

Discrete library

Description

The First-Order Hold block implements a first-order sample-and-hold that operates at the specified sampling interval. The block accepts one input and generates one output; both can be scalar or vector.

You can see the difference between the Zero-Order Hold and First-Order Hold blocks by entering fohdemo in the command window.

The following compares the output from a Sine Wave block and a First-Order Hold block:

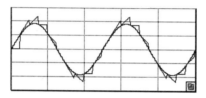

Parameters and Dialog Box

Sample Time

The time interval between samples. The sample time is specified as a scalar or a two-element vector. The first element is the sample time; the second element, if present, is the offset time. The offset time allows the sample hit to be offset from the end of the sample period. A positive offset specifies a lag; a negative offset specifies a lead for each sample hit.

```
┌──────────────────────────────────────────────────┐
│             First-Order Hold (Mask)                │
├──────────────────────────────────────────┬─────────┤
│ Block name:  First-Order Hold            │   OK    │
│ Block type:   First-Order Hold (Mask)    │         │
│ First-Order Hold                         │ Cancel  │
│                                          │         │
│                                          │  Help   │
│ Sample Time:                             │         │
│ ┌──────────────────────────────────────┐ │         │
│ │ 1│                                    │ │         │
│ └──────────────────────────────────────┘ │         │
└──────────────────────────────────────────┴─────────┘
```

Characteristics

Sample Time	Continuous
States	1 continuous, 1 discrete per input element
Direct Feedthrough	No

From File

untitled.mat ▷

Read data from a file   *Sources library*

Description

The From File block generates input by reading data from a specified file. The block displays the name of the file from which its data matrix is read.

The file must contain a matrix of at least two rows. The first row must contain monotonically increasing time points. Other rows contain data points corresponding to the time point in that column.

The block uses the time data to calculate its output, but does not include the time values in the output. This means that in a matrix containing m rows, the block outputs a vector of length $m-1$, consisting of data from all but the first row of the appropriate column.

If an output value is needed at a time that falls between two values in the file, the value is linearly interpolated between the time values that bracket the required time. The formula used to generate an output value, y, is

$$y = y_1 + \frac{(t-t_1)\ (y_2-y_1)}{(t_2-t_1)}$$

where t_1, t_2, y_1, and y_2 are the times and outputs nearest to the required time point t.

If the required time is less than the first time value or greater than the last time value in the file, SIMULINK extrapolates using the first two or last two points to compute a value. In both cases, the equation above is used.

Parameters and Dialog Box

Filename

The name of the file that contains the data used as input. The default file name is untitled.mat.

From File	
Block name: From File	OK
Block type: From File	
Reads row-wise matrix of time and output value(s) from data file. Interpolates for missing time.	Cancel
	Help
Filename:	
untitled.mat	

From File

Characteristics   Scalar Expansion   N/A
                       Sample Time   Inherited from driving block
                       States   0

From Workspace

Read data from a matrix defined in the workspace

Sources library

Description

The From Workspace block reads data from a matrix in the workspace. The block displays the name of the matrix or its time and input components.

The matrix must have two or more columns. The first column must contain monotonically increasing time points. Other columns contain data points that correspond to the time point in that row.

The block uses the time data to calculate its output, but does not include it in the output. Only data is output from the block. This means that for a matrix containing n columns, the block outputs a vector of length $n-1$, consisting of data from all but the first column of the appropriate row.

If an output value is needed at a time that falls between two values, the output is linearly interpolated between the two time values bracketing the required time. The formula used to generate an output value, y, is

$$y = y_1 + \frac{(t-t_1)(y_2-y_1)}{(t_2-t_1)}$$

where t_1, t_2, y_1, and y_2 are the nearest times and outputs to the required time point t.

If the required time is less than the first or greater than the last time value in the matrix, SIMULINK extrapolates using the first or last two points to compute a value. In both cases, the above equation is used.

Parameters and Dialog Box

Matrix table
The matrix from which time and data values are read. If these values are not in the same matrix, specify the time column vector T and data matrix U as [T,U]. If the values are in the same matrix, specify the matrix name. Avoid using ans to specify the data.

From Workspace	
Block name: From Workspace	OK
Block type: From Workspace	
Interpolates matrix of time and input values.Time must be in the first column.	Cancel
	Help
Matrix table:	
[T,U]	

From Workspace

Characteristics   Scalar Expansion   N/A
                        Sample Time   Inherited from driving block
                        States   0

Gain

Multiply block input

Linear library

Description

The Gain block generates its output by multiplying its input by a specified constant, variable, or expression.

If the input to the Gain block is a scalar, the gain must be specified as a scalar. The output is a scalar.

If the input to the Gain block is a vector, the output will be a vector of the same size. The gain can be either a scalar or a vector.

- If the gain is specified as a scalar, each element of the input vector is multiplied by the scalar gain to produce the corresponding element of the output vector.

- If the gain is specified as a vector, each element of the input vector is multipled by the corresponding element of the gain vector to produce an element of the output vector. In this case, the sizes of the gain and input vectors must be the same.

The Gain block displays the value entered in the **Gain** parameter field if the block is large enough. If the gain is specified as a variable, the block displays the variable name, although if the variable is specified in parentheses, the block evaluates the variable each time the block is redrawn and displays its value. If the Gain parameter value is too long to be displayed in the block, the string –K– is displayed.

Parameters and Dialog Box

Gain

The gain, specified as a scalar, vector, variable name, or expression. The default is 1.

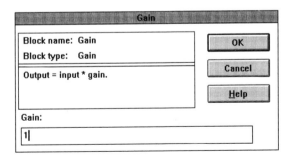

Characteristics

Scalar Expansion	Of **Gain** parameter
Sample Time	Inherited from driving block
States	0
Direct Feedthrough	Yes

Graph Scope

Display signals using MATLAB figure window   *Sinks library*

Description   The Graph Scope block plots its input in a MATLAB figure window.

The block accepts one input, which can be scalar or vector. The block plots the input with respect to simulation time. The plotting area is defined by the **Time range** parameter in the *x* direction and the **y-min** and **y-max** parameters in the *y* direction. Values outside the range in the *y* direction are not displayed.

If the input is a vector, the scope plots each signal according to colors, line types, and plot symbols specified by the **Line type** parameter.

Parameters and   **Time range**
Dialog Box   The range of the *x*-axis displayed in the graph window. When the simulation time exceeds the range, the scope is refreshed. The default is 20 seconds.

y-min
The minimum *y*-axis value. The default is -1.1.

y-max
The maximum *y*-axis value. The default is 1.2.

Line type
The color and line type or plot symbol for all output signals, enclosed in single quotation marks. Separate line types with a slash (/). For information about the codes, see the description of the MATLAB `plot` command. The default is `'y-/g--/c-./w:/m*/ro/b+'`.

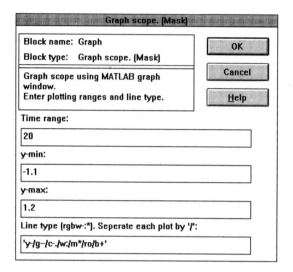

Graph scope. (Mask)

Block name: Graph

Block type: Graph scope. (Mask)

Graph scope using MATLAB graph
window.
Enter plotting ranges and line type.

[OK]

[Cancel]

[Help]

Time range:

20

y-min:

-1.1

y-max:

1.2

Line type (rgbw-:*). Seperate each plot by '/':

'y-/g--/c-./w:/m*/ro/b+'

Characteristics

Sample Time	Inherited from driving block
States	4 discrete (used internally for storage)

Hit Crossing

Increase the number of simulation steps around a specified value   *Sinks library*

Description

The Hit Crossing block increases the number of simulation steps when the input approaches a specified value. The block is useful for improving the accuracy of simulations of systems containing discontinuities. The block uses a resettable integrator and allows you to specify a tolerance to be used in the region specified by the **Crossing Value** parameter.

The Hit Crossing block should be connected to the signal that undergoes step discontinuity.

For a demo that illustrates the use of the Hit Crossing block, enter bounce in the command window.

The Euler integration technique may not detect the step discontinuity. Avoid using it with a model that includes a Hit Crossing block.

Parameters and Dialog Box

Crossing Value
The value at which the step discontinuity occurs. The default is 0.

Tolerance
The tolerance to be used around the **Crossing Value** parameter value. Smaller values enable the simulation to get within the minimum step size of the step discontinuity. When the minimum step size is activated, making the tolerance smaller has no effect. The default is 1e-6.

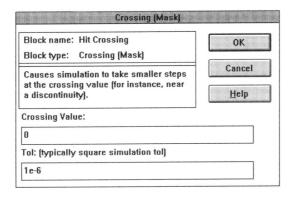

Characteristics

Scalar Expansion	Yes
Sample Time	Continuous
States	Inherited from driving block

Inner Product

Generate dot product   *Linear library*

Description   The Inner Product block generates the dot product of its two input vectors. The scalar output, y, is equal to the MATLAB operation

$$y = u1' * u2$$

where u1 and u2 represent the vector inputs. If the input vectors are not the same length, scalar expansion takes place.

To perform element-by-element multiplication without summing, use the Product block.

Dialog Box

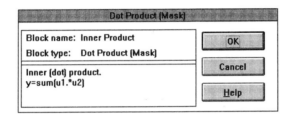

Characteristics | Sample Time | Inherited from driving block |
| --- | --- |
| States | 0 |
| Direct Feedthrough | Yes |

Inport

Provide a link to an external input and for linearization   *Connections library*

Description   Inports are the links from the outside world into a system.

For a subsystem, each input port on the subsystem block corresponds to an Inport block in the subsystem. A signal that arrives at an input port on a subsystem block flows out of the corresponding Inport within that block. SIMULINK automatically numbers the Inports within a subsystem sequentially, starting with 1. An added Inport block is assigned the first available number; for example, if existing Inports are numbered 1, 2, and 4, the next Inport is numbered 3. For more information about building subsystems, see "Creating Subsystems" in Chapter 3.

For a system that is not a subsystem, Inports represent external inputs for analysis functions, such as linmod, trim, and the integrators. They define the points where system inputs are injected into the systems. For information about using Inports for external inputs, see Chapter 4.

Inports at the top level support only scalar input, while at the subsystem level, they also support vector input.

Parameters and Dialog Box   **Port number**
The port number of the Inport. SIMULINK automatically assigns a port number to an Inport, although the port number can be changed.

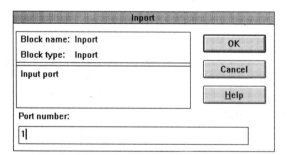

Characteristics   Sample Time   Inherited from driving block
States   0
Direct Feedthrough   Yes in subsystems

Integrator

Integrate a signal   *Linear library*

Description   The Integrator block integrates its input. The output of the integrator is simply its state, the integral.

The input to the Integrator block can be a scalar or vector. The output size matches the input.

Parameters and Dialog Box

Initial value
The initial condition, which can be specified as a constant or a variable.

If the input is a vector and the initial value is specified as a vector, they must be the same size. If the initial value is specified as a scalar, scalar expansion takes place. The m-th element of the input vector is integrated with the initial value specified by the m-th element of the initial value vector to produce the m-th element in the output vector.

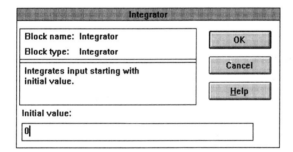

Characteristics

Scalar Expansion	Of the **Initial value** parameter
Sample Time	Continuous
States	Number of inputs
Direct Feedthrough	No

Limited Integrator

Integrate within specified bounds

Nonlinear library

Description

The Limited Integrator block prevents the output of an Integrator block from exceeding specified levels. The block output is determined as follows:

- When the integral is less than the **Lower bound** parameter value, the output is the **Lower bound**.
- When the integral is between the **Lower bound** and the **Upper bound** parameter values, the output is the integral.
- When the integral is greater than the **Upper bound** parameter value, the output is the **Upper bound**.

This block is designed so that when the integral is outside the lower and upper bounds, the integral action is turned off to prevent integral wind up.

The block accepts one input and generates one output, both of which can be scalar or vector.

Parameters and Dialog Box

Lower bound
The minimum integral value.

Upper bound
The maximum integral value

Initial condition
The initial condition, which can be entered as a constant or a variable. If the input is a vector and the initial value is specified as a vector, they must be the same size. If the initial value is specified as a scalar, scalar expansion takes place. The m-th element of the input vector is integrated with the initial value specified by the m-th element of the initial value vector to produce the m-th element in the output vector.

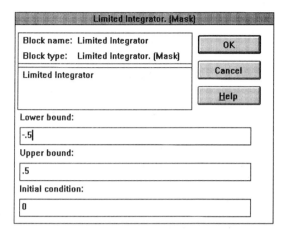

Characteristics   Scalar Expansion   Of parameters
                      Sample Time   Continuous
                      States   Parameters or inherited from driving block
                      Direct Feedthrough   No

Logical Operator

Perform specified logical operation on the input　　　　*Nonlinear library*

Description　　　The Logical Operator block performs any one of the following logical operations on its inputs: AND, NAND, OR, NOR, NOT, and XOR. Each input can be a scalar or vector. The output depends on the number of inputs, their vector size, and the operator. The specified operator is displayed on the block icon.

- For two or more inputs, the block performs the operation between all of the inputs. If the inputs are vectors, the operation is performed between corresponding elements of the vectors to produce a vector output.

- For a single vector input, the block applies the operation to all elements of that vector except the NOT operator.

  The NOT operator accepts only one input, which can be a scalar or vector. If the input is a vector, the output is a vector of the same size containing the logical complements of the elements of the input vector.

A nonzero input is treated as TRUE (1); a zero input as FALSE (0). The output is 1 if TRUE and 0 if FALSE.

When configured as a multi-input XOR gate, this block performs an addition modulo two operation as mandated by the IEEE Standard for Logic Elements.

Parameters and Dialog Box

Operator
The logical operator to be applied to the block inputs. Valid entries are the operators listed above, those provided by MATLAB and the C programming language, and the symbols of the IEEE Standard for Logic Elements.

Number of Input Ports
The number of block inputs.

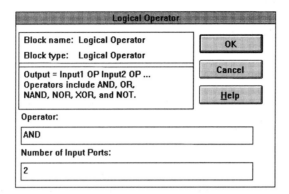

Characteristics

Scalar Expansion	Of inputs
Sample Time	Inherited from driving block
States	0
Direct Feedthrough	Yes

Look-Up Table

Perform piecewise linear mapping of the input   *Nonlinear library*

Description   The Look-Up Table block implements piecewise linear mapping of the input into a table defined by the block's parameters.

You define the table by specifying (either as row or column vectors) the **Vector of input values** and **Vector of output values** parameters. The block produces an output value by comparing the block input with values in the input vector:

- If it finds a value that matches the block's input, the output is the corresponding element in the output vector.

- If it does not find a value that matches, it performs linear interpolation between the two appropriate elements of the table to determine an output value. If the block input is less than the first or greater than the last input vector element, the block extrapolates from the first or last two points.

To create a table with step transitions, specify an input value twice, once for each output value for the same input point. For example, if you specify these input and output parameters:

```
Vector of input values:     [0 1 1 2]
Vector of output values:    [-1 -1 1 1]
```

the block creates an input/output relationship described by this plot:

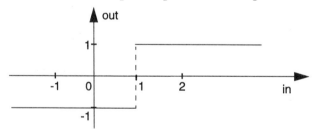

These values generate -1 for inputs less than 1 and +1 for inputs greater than 1.

The Look-Up Table block displays a graph of the input vector versus the output vector on its icon. When a parameter is changed on the block's dialog box, the graph is automatically redrawn when you press the **OK** button to close the dialog box.

Parameters and Dialog Box

Vector of input values

The vector of values containing possible block input values. This vector must be the same size as the output vector. The input vector must be monotonically increasing.

Vector of output values

The vector of values containing block output values. This vector must be the same size as the input vector.

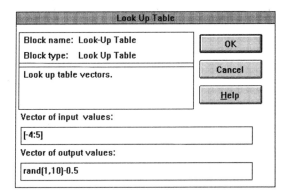

Characteristics

Scalar Expansion	Of parameters
Sample Time	Inherited from driving block
States	0
Direct Feedthrough	Yes

MATLAB Fcn

Apply a MATLAB function to the input   *Nonlinear library*

Description
The MATLAB Fcn block applies the specified MATLAB function or expression to the input. The block accepts one input, which can be scalar or vector. The specified function or expression is applied to the input vector, and the output is formatted according to the specified output width. These expressions are valid for this block:

```
sin
atan2(u(1), u(2))
u(1)^u(2)
```

> This block is very inefficient because it calls the MATLAB parser at each integration step. Consider using built-in blocks instead or writing the function as an M-file and accessing it using the Fcn block.

Parameters and Dialog Box

MATLAB function
The function or expression. If you specify a function only, it is not necessary to include the input argument in parentheses. For example, if the specified function is sin, the output is sin(u), where u is the input.

Output width
The output width. If the output width is to be the same as the input width, specify –1. Otherwise, you must specify the correct width or a runtime error will result.

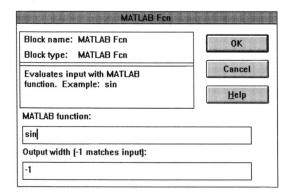

Characteristics

Sample Time	Inherited from driving block
States	0
Direct Feedthrough	Yes

Matrix Gain

Multiply input by a matrix   *Linear library*

Description

The Matrix Gain block implements a matrix gain. It generates its output by multiplying its vector input by a specified matrix:

$$y = Ku$$

where K is the gain and u is the input.

If the specified matrix has m rows and n columns, then the input to this block should be a vector of length n. The output is a vector of length m.

Parameters and Dialog Box

Gain matrix
The gain, specified as a matrix.

```
┌─────────────────────────────────────────────┐
│              Matrix Gain (Mask)              │
├─────────────────────────────────────────────┤
│ ┌──────────────────────────┐  ┌───────────┐ │
│ │ Block name: Matrix Gain  │  │    OK     │ │
│ │ Block type:  Matrix Gain (Mask)          │
│ ├──────────────────────────┤  ┌───────────┐ │
│ │ Matrix Gain.             │  │  Cancel   │ │
│ │                          │  └───────────┘ │
│ │                          │  ┌───────────┐ │
│ └──────────────────────────┘  │   Help    │ │
│ Gain matrix:                  └───────────┘ │
│ ┌─────────────────────────────────────────┐ │
│ │ eye(3,3)                                 │ │
│ └─────────────────────────────────────────┘ │
└─────────────────────────────────────────────┘
```

Characteristics

Scalar Expansion	No
Sample Time	Inherited from driving block
States	0
Direct Feedthrough	Yes

Memory

Output the block input at the previous integration step   *Nonlinear library*

Description   The Memory block ouputs its input from the previous major integration step, applying a one integration step sample-and-hold to its input signal. The block accepts one input and generates one output, both of which can be scalar or vector. This block can be used for removing algebraic loops. For more information, see "Algebraic Loops" in Chapter 4.

For example, this model demonstrates how to display the step size used in a simulation:

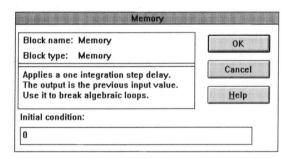

The Sum block subtracts the time at the previous step, generated by the Memory block, from the current time generated by the clock.

Parameters and Dialog Box   **Initial condition**
The output at the initial integration step. If necessary, SIMULINK applies scalar expansion to match the size of the input vector.

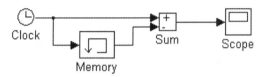

Characteristics

Sample Time	Continuous
States	0
Direct Feedthrough	No

Mux

Combine several input lines into a vector line   *Connections library*

Description   The Mux block combines several input lines into one vector line. The block accepts a specifiable number of input lines, which can be scalars and/or vectors. The output of a Mux block is a vector.

SIMULINK draws the Mux block input ports to reflect the specified number of inputs, resizing the block if necessary.

Parameters and Dialog Box

Number of Inputs

The number and width of inputs. The total of the input widths must match the width of the output line.

Generally, specify the number of input ports. SIMULINK determines their widths by checking the output ports of the blocks feeding the Mux block.

If it is necessary to explicitly specify any or all of the input widths, you can specify them as a vector. Include elements with -1 values for those inputs whose widths are to be determined dynamically (during the simulation).

For example, [4 1 2] indicates three inputs forming a seven-element output vector: the first four output elements are from the first input, the fifth element comes from the second input, and the sixth and seventh elements come from the third input. If it is not important that these inputs have fixed widths, you could specify the **Number of Inputs** as 3.

To specify three inputs where the first input vector must have four elements, you could specify [4 -1 -1]. SIMULINK determines the widths of the second and third inputs and sizes the output width accordingly.

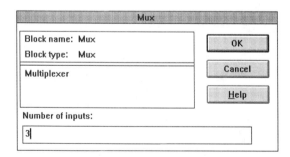

Characteristics   Sample Time   Inherited from driving block
                       States   0
                       Direct Feedthrough   Yes

Outport

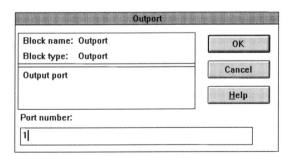

Provide a link to an external output and for linearization   *Connections library*

Description   Outports are the links from a system to the outside world.

For a subsystem, each output port on the subsystem block corresponds to an Outport in the subsystem. A signal that arrives at an Outport block flows out of the corresponding output port on the subsystem block. SIMULINK automatically numbers Outports within a subsystem sequentially, starting with 1. An added Outport block is assigned the first available number; for example, if existing ports are numbered 1, 2, and 4, the next port is numbered 3. For information about building subsystems, see "Creating Subsystems" in Chapter 3.

For a system that is not a subsystem, Outports define system outputs for analysis functions, such as linmod, trim, and the integrators. For more information about using Outports in this way, see Chapter 4.

If two or more Outport blocks are included when you group blocks together to create a new subsystem block, the ports on the Outport blocks are renumbered automatically. When you open that subsystem block, the port numbers may be different than they were in the original block diagram.

Outports at the top level support only scalar output, while at the subsystem level, they also support vector input.

Parameters and   **Port number**
Dialog Box   The port number of the Outport. SIMULINK automatically assigns a port number to an Outport, although the port number can be changed.

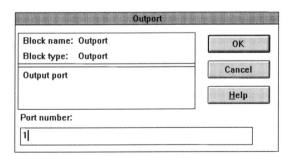

Characteristics   Sample Time   Inherited from driving block
                         States   0
                         Direct Feedthrough   Yes in subsystems

Product

Multiply inputs together   *Nonlinear library*

Description   The Product block multiplies the value of each input to produce its output. Inputs can be scalars or vectors. You can use the block to multiply scalars, multiply vectors, multiply one or more vectors by the same scalar value, and multiply the elements of a single vector:

- With scalar inputs, the output is the product of the inputs.
- With vector inputs, the output is a vector that is the element by element product of all the input vectors. All vectors must be the same size.
- With scalar and vector inputs, SIMULINK applies scalar expansion to expand automatically each scalar to a vector of the appropriate length, with identical elements. The output is a vector that is the element by element product of the inputs.
- When driven by a single vector input, the Product block multiplies all the elements in the input vector. In this case, the Π symbol is displayed on the block icon.

If necessary, SIMULINK resizes the block to show all input ports.

Parameters and   **Number of Inputs**
Dialog Box   The number of inputs to the block.

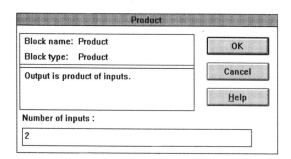

Characteristics   Sample Time   Inherited from driving block
                      States   0
                      Direct Feedthrough   Yes

Pulse Generator

Generate pulses at regular intervals   *Sources library*

Description The Pulse Generator block creates a series of pulses at regular intervals. Because it is important that the integration routine "sees" the pulses as they are generated, this block contains several discrete-time blocks to guarantee that the integrator does not skip over and ignore (or truncate) the pulses. The block generates one scalar output.

Parameters and Dialog Box

Pulse period
The pulse period in seconds. The default is three seconds.

Pulse width
The pulse width. The default is two seconds.

Pulse height
The pulse height. If specified as a vector, the block generates a vector of pulses. The default is 1.

Pulse start time
The delay before the pulse is generated, in seconds. The default is 0.5 seconds.

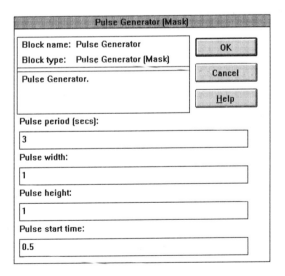

Pulse Generator (Mask)	
Block name: Pulse Generator	OK
Block type: Pulse Generator (Mask)	Cancel
Pulse Generator.	Help

Pulse period (secs):

`3`

Pulse width:

`1`

Pulse height:

`1`

Pulse start time:

`0.5`

Characteristics   Sample Time   Continuous
                      Discrete States   Yes (associated with the Unit Delay blocks used)

Quantizer

Discretize input at a specified interval   *Nonlinear library*

Description   The Quantizer block passes its input signal through a stair-step function
so that many neighboring points on the input axis are mapped to one point
on the output axis. The effect is to quantize a smooth signal into a stair-
step output. The output is computed using the roundoff or round-to-nearest
method, which produces an output that is symmetric about zero:

    y = q * round(u/q)

where y is the output, u the input, and q the **Quantization Interval** parameter. Input and output can be scalar or vector.

Parameters and   **Quantization Interval**
Dialog Box   The interval, around which the output is quantized. Permissible output
values for the Quantizer block are $n*q$, where n is an integer and q the
Quantization Interval.

```
                    Quantizer (Mask)

   Block name:  Quantizer                    ┌──────────┐
                                             │    OK    │
   Block type:   Quantizer (Mask)            └──────────┘

   Discretizes input at given interval.      ┌──────────┐
                                             │  Cancel  │
                                             └──────────┘

                                             ┌──────────┐
                                             │   Help   │
                                             └──────────┘
   Quantization interval:

   0.5
```

Characteristics   Scalar Expansion   Of parameter
Sample Time   Inherited from driving block
States   0
Direct Feedthrough   Yes

Random Number

Generate normally distributed random numbers   *Sources library*

Description

The Random Number block generates normally distributed random numbers. It generates the same sequence of random numbers as MATLAB's randn function for any given starting seed value. The seed is reset to the specified value each time a simulation starts.

The Random Number block is a pseudorandom, normally distributed (Gaussian) number generator. The sequence produced has a mean of zero and a variance of one. This sequence is repeatable and can be produced by any Random Number block with the same seed. To generate a vector of random numbers, specify the **Initial seed** parameter as a vector of seeds.

You should not use this block with continuous-time systems because of numerical issues. Instead, use the Band-Limited White Noise block.

Parameters and Dialog Box

Initial Seed

Used to generate random numbers. If specified as a vector, the block generates a vector of random noise signals. The default is 0.

White Noise	
Block name: Random Number	OK
Block type: White Noise	
Random sequence is repeatable for a given seed. Output is normally distributed.	Cancel
	Help
Initial Seed:	
0	

Characteristics

Sample Time	Inherited from driving block
States	0

Rate Limiter

Limit the rate of change of a signal   *Nonlinear library*

Description   The Rate Limiter block limits the first derivative of the signal passing through it. The output changes no faster than the specified limit. The derivative is calculated using the following equation:

$$rate = \frac{\Delta u}{\Delta t} = \frac{u(i) - y(i-1)}{t(i) - t(i-1)}$$

where $u(i)$ and $t(i)$ are the current input and time and $y(i-1)$ and $t(i-1)$ are the output of the block and time from the previous step. The block output is determined by comparing *rate* to the block parameters, **Rising slew rate** and **Falling slew rate**:

- If *rate* is greater than the absolute value of the **Rising slew rate** parameter, the output is calculated as:

$$y(i) = \Delta t(abs(R)) + y(i-1)$$

where $y(i)$ is the current output of the block and R is the rising slew rate.

- If *rate* is less than the **Falling slew rate** parameter, the output is calculated as:

$$y(i) = -\Delta t(abs(F)) + y(i-1)$$

where F is the falling slew rate.

- If *rate* is between the bounds of R and F, the output is computed by projecting a line with slope *rate* from the last input:

$$y(i) = \Delta t \cdot rate + y(i-1)$$

The block accepts one input and generates one output, both of which can be scalar or vector.

Parameters and   **Rising slew rate**
Dialog Box   The limit of the derivative of an increasing input signal. This parameter can be a vector for a vector input, or a scalar.

Falling slew rate
The limit of the derivative of a decreasing input signal. This parameter can be a vector for a vector input, or a scalar.

```
┌─────────────────────────────────────────────────────┐
│                    Rate Limiter                      │
├─────────────────────────────────────┬───────────────┤
│ Block name:  Rate Limiter           │   ┌────────┐   │
│ Block type:    Rate Limiter         │   │   OK   │   │
├─────────────────────────────────────┤   └────────┘   │
│ Rate limits.                        │   ┌────────┐   │
│                                     │   │ Cancel │   │
│                                     │   └────────┘   │
│                                     │   ┌────────┐   │
│                                     │   │  Help  │   │
├─────────────────────────────────────┴───┴────────┴───┤
│ Rising slew rate:                                    │
│ ┌─────────────────────────────────────────────────┐ │
│ │ 1│                                               │ │
│ └─────────────────────────────────────────────────┘ │
│ Falling slew rate:                                   │
│ ┌─────────────────────────────────────────────────┐ │
│ │ -1                                               │ │
│ └─────────────────────────────────────────────────┘ │
└─────────────────────────────────────────────────────┘
```

Characteristics

Scalar Expansion	Of parameters
Sample Time	Inherited from driving block
States	0
Direct Feedthrough	Yes

Relational Operator

Perform specified relational operation on the input   *Nonlinear library*

Description   The Relational Operator block performs a relational operation on its two inputs and produces output according to the following table:

Operator	Output
==	TRUE if the first input is equal to the second input
!=	TRUE if the first input is not equal to the second input
<	TRUE if the first input is less than the second input
<=	TRUE if the first input is less than or equal to the second input
>=	TRUE if the first input is greater than or equal to the second input
>	TRUE if the first input is greater than the second input

If the result is TRUE, the output is 1; if FALSE, it is 0. You can specify inputs as scalars, vectors, or a combination of a scalar and a vector:

- For scalar inputs, the output is a scalar.

- For vector inputs, the output is a vector, where each element is the result of an element by element comparison of the input vectors.

- For mixed scalar/vector inputs, the output is a vector, where each element is the result of a comparison between the scalar and the corresponding vector element.

The specified operator is displayed in the block icon.

Parameters and   **Operator**
Dialog Box   The relational operator to be applied to the block inputs. You can specify only one operator regardless of the width of the inputs.

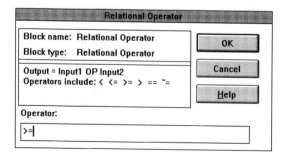

Characteristics

Scalar Expansion	Of inputs
Sample Time	Inherited from driving block
States	0
Direct Feedthrough	Yes

Relay

Switch output between two values

Nonlinear library

Description

The Relay block allows the output to switch between two specified values. When the relay is on, it remains on until the input drops below the specified value of the **Input for off** parameter. When the relay is off, it remains off until the input exceeds the specified value of the **Input for on** parameter.

The block accepts one input and generates one output, both of which can be scalar or vector.

Parameters and Dialog Box

Input for on
The "on" threshold for the relay. When the input exceeds this value, the relay is on. Specifying an **Input for on** value greater than the **Input for off** value models hysteresis, whereas specifying equal values models a switch with a threshold at that value.

Input for off
The "off" threshold for the relay. When the input falls below this value, the relay is off. **Input for off** greater than **Input for on** is an undefined case and causes the output of the relay to "chatter" between its two preset output values at the rate of the system simulation, changing state with every step taken by the simulator whenever the input value falls between the **Input for on** and **Input for off** values.

Output when on
The output value when the relay is on.

Output when off
The output value when the relay is off.

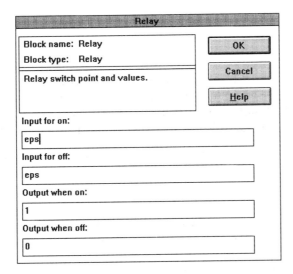

Characteristics

Scalar Expansion	Of parameters
Sample Time	Inherited from driving block
States	0
Direct Feedthrough	Yes

Repeating Sequence

Generate a regularly repeatable arbitrary signal

Sources library

Description
The Repeating Sequence block allows you to specify an arbitrary signal to be repeated regularly over time. This block is implemented using the one-dimensional Look-Up Table block, performing linear interpolation between points.

The block generates one scalar output.

Parameters and Dialog Box

Time values
A vector of monotonically increasing time values. The default is [0 2 2].

Output values
A vector of output values. Each corresponds to the time value in the same column. The default is [0 2 0].

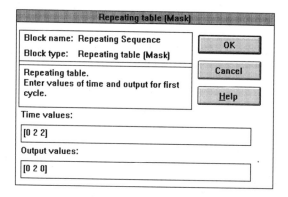

Characteristics

Sample Time	Continuous
States	0

Reset Integrator

Reset integrator states during simulation   *Nonlinear library*

Description   The Reset Integrator block is an Integrator block whose states can be reset during a simulation. The block has three inputs:

- Signal
- Control or reset, a logical expression that, when evaluated to TRUE (or when it has a nonzero value), causes the block to reset its states
- Initial values of states when reset

The block integrates the signal input while the control input is zero. When the control input becomes nonzero, the block resets its states to the values of the third input, then integrates the signal beginning immediately afterward. The block checks the control input only at major integration steps; at minor steps, it continues integrating the signal, functioning as an Integrator block (described on page 145). To stop integration during resetting, put logic on the first input. To see a masked block that does this, open the resetint system. Integration major and minor steps are described in "Controlling the Step Size" in Chapter 4.

The inputs and the single output can be scalar or vector.

A demo shows this block used in a model of a bouncing ball. To run the demo, enter bounce in the MATLAB command window. In this model, the Reset Integrator block integrates its first input (gravity) to generate the ball's velocity. An Integrator block generates the ball's position. A Fcn block determines when the ball's velocity is negative and its position is either very close to zero or negative. When both conditions are TRUE, the Reset Integrator block's state is reset to -0.8 times its previous value, which indicates a change in direction and a loss of energy.

Parameters and   **Initial value**
Dialog Box   The output of the block at the first integration step if the control input is zero at the start of the simulation. (If the control input is nonzero, the block uses the value at the third input port.) You can specify this parameter as a scalar or vector; if a vector, its size must match the width of any vector inputs.

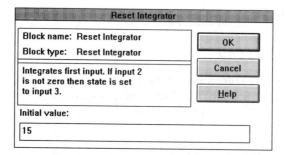

Characteristics

Scalar Expansion	Of inputs and the **Initial value** parameter
Sample Time	Continuous
States	Inherited from driving block or **Initial value** parameter
Direct Feedthrough	No

Saturation

Limit excursion of a signal   *Nonlinear library*

Description   The Saturation block imposes upper and lower bounds on a signal. Within the range specified by the **Lower output limit** and **Upper output limit** parameters, the input signal passes through unchanged. Outside these bounds, the signal is clipped to the maximum or minimum bound.

When the parameters are set to the same value, the block constantly outputs that value. When the **Upper output value** is less than the **Lower output value**, the block outputs the lower value.

The block accepts one input and generates one output, both of which can be scalar or vector.

Parameters and   **Lower output limit**
Dialog Box   The lower bound on the input signal. While the signal is below this value, the output is set to this value.

Upper output limit
The upper bound on the input signal. While the signal is above this value, the output is set to this value.

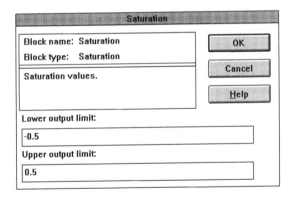

Characteristics   Scalar Expansion   Of parameters
                       Sample Time   Inherited from driving block
                       States   0
                       Direct Feedthrough   Yes

Scope

Display signals during simulation

Sinks library

Description

The Scope block displays its input with respect to simulation time. The block accepts one input, which can be scalar or vector. The Scope allows you to adjust the amount of time and the range of input values displayed. You can move and resize the Scope window although reducing its size may lose the horizontal and vertical range parameter fields and the **OK** button.

A Scope block whose input is unconnected is called a *floating Scope*. It displays the activity of any line selected by the mouse. This can be useful for quickly looking at the behavior of a system at different points.

When you start a simulation, SIMULINK does not open Scope windows. You can modify the block's parameter values during the simulation.

Parameters and Dialog Box

Vertical range

The range of values that can be displayed in the positive and negative directions on the scope. As the figures show, the full range of values that can be displayed is twice the **Vertical range** parameter value.

Horizontal range

The number of seconds of output displayed before the scope gets refreshed.

The Scope window on a Windows system appears below. The figure labels the origin and the horizontal and vertical ranges.

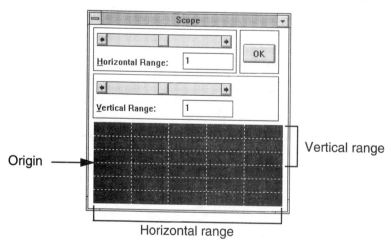

You can set the vertical and horizontal ranges by entering numeric values in the appropriate fields. Specify the horizontal range in seconds; the vertical range has no units.

You can also set the vertical and horizontal ranges using the sliders. The slider indicator position always matches the value displayed in the field and the lower limit is always 0. If you change a value, the slider indicator remains in the same position but the range of values you can get using the slider changes. For example, if the slider indicator is in the center of the slider and the value displayed in the field is 1, the range of values you can get using the slider is from 0 to 2. If you change the value in the field to 5, the slider indicator doesn't move but now the range of values you can get using the slider changes from 0 to 10.

The Scope window on a Macintosh system appears below. The figure labels the origin and the vertical and horizontal ranges. You can turn the horizontal and vertical grid lines on and off by clicking in the check boxes.

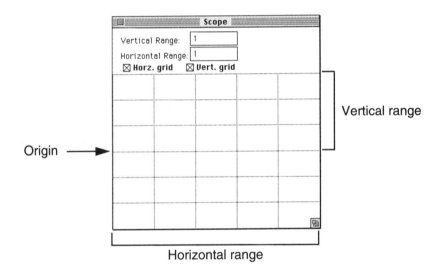

Characteristics	Sample Time	Inherited from driving block
	States	0

Sign

Return the sign of the input   *Nonlinear library*

Description   The Sign block outputs the sign of the input, as follows:

- The output is 1 when the input is greater than zero.
- The output is 0 when the input is equal to zero.
- The output is -1 when the input is less than zero.

The input and output can be scalar or vector.

Dialog Box

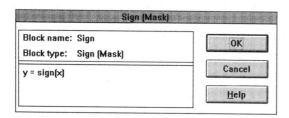

Characteristics   Sample Time   Inherited from driving block
                        States   0
                        Direct Feedthrough   Yes

Signal Generator

Generate various waveforms   *Sources library*

Description   The Signal Generator block can produce one of four different waveforms: sine wave, square wave, sawtooth wave, and random noise.

**Parameters and
Dialog Box**

Frequency
Specify the frequency by entering a value in the field or by using the slider. On a Windows system, the frequency is in radians per second. On the Macintosh, you can specify frequency in either radians per second or Hz. You can only enter a number, not a variable name, in this field. The default is 1 rad/sec. You can specify the range of values selectable with the slider by entering a number in the **Range** field.

Peak (or **Amplitude**)
You can specify the peak or amplitude by entering a value in the field or by using the slider. You can only enter a number, not a variable name, in this field. The default is 1. You can specify the range of values selectable with the slider by entering a number in the **Range** field.

The Windows dialog box for this block appears below.

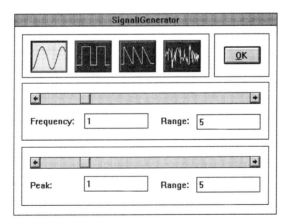

The Macintosh version of the dialog box appears below.

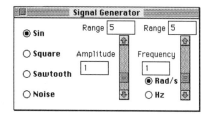

You can vary the output settings of the Signal Generator block while a simulation is in progress, which is particularly effective when the response of a system to different types of inputs needs to be ascertained quickly.

You cannot adjust the phase of the Signal Generator output. You can generate a phase-shifted sine wave using the Sine Wave block. You can generate a precisely timed rising or falling edge with the Step Input block. You can generate a phase-shifted square, sine, or sawtooth wave in a variety of ways, including inputting a Clock block signal to a MATLAB Fcn block and writing the equation for the particular wave.

The random noise button (the right-most signal button on the Windows dialog box and the **Noise** radio button on the Macintosh dialog box) produces uniformly distributed noise using the C language's random number generator function. To get normally distributed noise, use the Random Number block.

The Signal Generator block outputs a scalar value only.

Characteristics

Sample Time	Inherited from driving block
States	0

Sine Wave

Generate a sine wave   *Sources library*

Description   The Sine Wave block provides a time varying sinusoid. The block can operate in either continuous or discrete mode.

The output of the Sine Wave block is determined by:

$$y = Amplitude \times \sin(frequency \times time + phase)$$

The Sine Wave block generates scalar or vector output.

Using the Sine Wave Block in Discrete Mode

If you set the **Sample Time** parameter to a nonzero value, the block behaves as if it were driving a Zero-Order Hold block whose sample time is set to that value.

Using the Sine Wave block in this way allows you to build models with sine wave sources that are purely discrete, rather than models that are hybrid continuous/discrete systems. Hybrid systems are inherently more complex and, as a result, take longer to simulate.

Using the Sine Wave Block in Continuous Mode

When operating in continuous mode, the Sine Wave block can become inaccurate due to loss of precision as time t becomes very large. The Sine Wave block in discrete mode circumvents this problem by using an incremental algorithm rather than one based on absolute time. As a result, it can be useful in models intended to run for an indefinite length of time, such as in vibration or fatigue testing.

The incremental algorithm computes the sine based on the value computed at the previous sample time. This method makes use of the following identities:

$$\sin(t + \Delta t) = \sin(t)\cos(\Delta t) + \sin(\Delta t)\cos(t)$$
$$\cos(t + \Delta t) = \cos(t)\cos(\Delta t) - \sin(t)\sin(\Delta t)$$

These identities can be written in matrix form:

$$\begin{bmatrix} \sin(t + \Delta t) \\ \cos(t + \Delta t) \end{bmatrix} = \begin{bmatrix} \cos(\Delta t) & \sin(\Delta t) \\ -\sin(\Delta t) & \cos(\Delta t) \end{bmatrix} \begin{bmatrix} \sin(t) \\ \cos(t) \end{bmatrix}$$

Since Δt is constant, the following expression is a constant.

$$\begin{bmatrix} \cos{(\Delta t)} & \sin{(\Delta t)} \\ -\sin{(\Delta t)} & \cos{(\Delta t)} \end{bmatrix}$$

Therefore the problem becomes one of a matrix multiply of the value of $\sin{(t)}$ by a constant matrix to obtain $\sin{(t + \Delta t)}$. This algorithm may also be faster on machines that do not have hardware floating-point support for trigonometric functions.

Parameters and Dialog Box

Amplitude
The amplitude of the signal. The default is 1.

Frequency
The frequency, in radians/second. The default is 1 rad/sec.

Phase
The phase shift, in radians. The default is 0 radians.

Sample Time
When you specify a nonzero value for the **Sample Time** parameter, the block become discrete. See the discussion above for the use of the block in discrete mode. The default is 0.

Sine Wave	
Block name: Sine Wave	OK
Block type: Sine Wave	Cancel
ZOH(Amp*sin(Freq*Time+Phase))	Help

Amplitude:

`1`

Frequency (rads/sec):

`1`

Phase (rads):

`0`

Sample Time: (Zero or empty for continuous)

Characteristics

Scalar Expansion	Of parameters
Sample Time	Continuous or discrete
States	0

Slider Gain

Vary a scalar gain using a slider

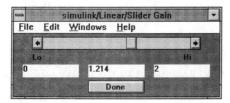

Linear library

Description

The Slider Gain block allows you to vary a scalar gain during a simulation using a slider. The block accepts one input and generates one output, both of which can be scalar or vector. If the input is a vector, the gain is scalar expanded and applied to each element of the input vector.

Dialog Box

The dialog box contains the slider, text fields, and a **Done** button. The text fields indicate (from left to right) the lower limit, the current value, and the upper limit. You can change the gain in two ways: by manipulating the slider or by entering a new value in the current value field. Close the dialog box by clicking on the **Done** button.

If you click on a slider arrow, the current value changes by about 1% of the slider's range. If you click on a trough (the rectangular area to either side of the slider's indicator), the current value changes by about 10% of the slider's range.

Characteristics

Scalar Expansion	Of the gain
Sample Time	Inherited from driving block
States	0
Direct Feedthrough	Yes

State-Space

```
┌──────────────┐
│  x' = Ax+Bu  │
│  y  = Cx+Du  │
└──────────────┘
```

Implement a linear state-space system   *Linear library*

Description   The State-Space block implements a system whose behavior is defined by:

$$\dot{x} = Ax + Bu$$
$$y = Cx + Du$$

where x is the state vector, u is the input vector, and y is the output vector.

The block accepts one input and generates one output, both of which can be scalar or vector.

Parameters and Dialog Box

A, B, C, D
The matrix coefficients as defined in the above equations.

• **A** must be an n-by-n matrix, where n is the number of states.

• **B** must be an n-by-m matrix, where m is the number of inputs.

• **C** must be a r-by-n matrix, where r is the number of outputs.

• **D** must be a r-by-m matrix.

Initial conditions
The initial state vector. If not supplied, it is assumed to be zero.

```
┌─────────────────────────────────────────────────────────┐
│                      State-Space                         │
├───────────────────────────────────────┬─────────────────┤
│  Block name:  State-Space              │   ┌─────────┐   │
│  Block type:    State-Space            │   │   OK    │   │
│                                        │   └─────────┘   │
│  State-space model matrices:           │   ┌─────────┐   │
│    dx/dt = Ax + Bu                     │   │ Cancel  │   │
│    y = Cx + Du                         │   └─────────┘   │
│                                        │   ┌─────────┐   │
│                                        │   │  Help   │   │
│  A:                                    │   └─────────┘   │
│  ┌──────────────────────────────────────────────────┐   │
│  │ 1│                                                │   │
│  └──────────────────────────────────────────────────┘   │
│  B:                                                      │
│  ┌──────────────────────────────────────────────────┐   │
│  │ 1                                                  │   │
│  └──────────────────────────────────────────────────┘   │
│  C:                                                      │
│  ┌──────────────────────────────────────────────────┐   │
│  │ 1                                                  │   │
│  └──────────────────────────────────────────────────┘   │
│  D:                                                      │
│  ┌──────────────────────────────────────────────────┐   │
│  │ 1                                                  │   │
│  └──────────────────────────────────────────────────┘   │
│  Initial conditions:                                     │
│  ┌──────────────────────────────────────────────────┐   │
│  │                                                    │   │
│  └──────────────────────────────────────────────────┘   │
└─────────────────────────────────────────────────────────┘
```

Characteristics

Sample Time	Continuous
States	Variable, size of A
Direct Feedthrough	Only if $D \neq 0$

Step Input

Generate a step function   *Sources library*

Description   The Step Input block provides a step between two arbitrary levels at a specified time. If the simulation time is less than the **Step time** parameter value, the block's output is the **Initial value** parameter value. For simulation time greater than or equal to the **Step time**, the output is the **Final value** parameter value.

The Step Input block generates one scalar or vector output, depending on the size of the parameters.

Parameters and   **Step time**
Dialog Box   The time in seconds when the output jumps from the **Initial value** parameter to the **Final value** parameter. The default is one second.

Initial value
The block output until the simulation time reaches the **Step time** parameter value. The default is 0.

Final value
The block output when the simulation time reaches and exceeds the **Step time** parameter value. The default is 1.

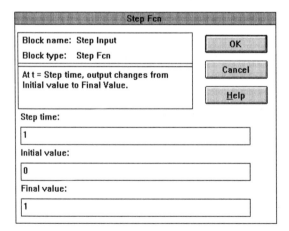

Characteristics   Scalar Expansion   Of parameters
Sample Time   Inherited from driving block
States   0

Stop Simulation

Stop simulation when input is nonzero

Sinks library

Description

The Stop Simulation block stops the simulation when the input is nonzero.

The Stop Simulation block allows the immediate termination of a simulation whenever the input to this block is nonzero. The block can accept a scalar or vector input.

You can use this block in conjunction with the Relational Operator block to control when the simulation stops. When this block is used in conjunction with the Derivative block, it is possible to stop the simulation on rising or falling crossing points.

Dialog Box

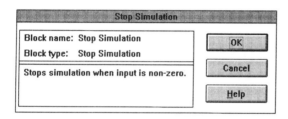

Characteristics

Sample Time	Inherited from driving block
States	0

Subsystem

Represent a system within another system　　　　　　　　　*Connections*

Description　　A Subsystem block represents a system within another system. A set of blocks and lines can be converted to a Subsystem block by selecting the objects using a bounding box, then choosing the **Group** command on the **Options** menu. For more information about creating subsystems, see "Creating Subsystems" in Chapter 3.

When you create a subsystem, lines connected to blocks outside the subsystem are replaced in the subsystem with inports and outports, respectively. The number of input ports drawn on the Subsystem block's icon corresponds to the number of inports contained in the subsystem. The top input connects to inport 1, the next input connects to inport 2, and so on. The output ports drawn on the block correspond in the same way to the number of outports contained in the subsystem.

Changes to the number of inports and outports in the subsystem cause the block to be redrawn immediately with the correct numbers of input and output ports. If necessary, SIMULINK resizes the block.

Dialog Box　　None

Characteristics　　
Scalar Expansion	Variable
Sample Time	Variable
States	Variable
Direct Feedthrough	Variable

Sum

Generate the sum of inputs   *Linear library*

Description

The Sum block adds the value of each input to produce its output.

Use the block to add scalars, add vectors, add the same scalar value to one or more vectors, and add the elements of a single vector.

- Adding Scalars

  With scalar inputs, the output is the algebraic sum of the inputs.

- Adding Vectors

  With vector inputs, the vector output is the element by element sum of all the input vectors.

- Adding the Same Scalar Value to Vectors

  With scalar and vector inputs, the block applies scalar expansion. Each scalar input is automatically expanded to a vector of the appropriate length, with identical elements.

- Adding the Elements of a Single Vector

  When driven by a single vector input, the block adds all the elements in the input vector to generate a scalar output. In this case, the block changes its icon to a Σ.

The Sum block draws plus and minus signs beside the appropriate ports and redraws its ports to match the number of signs specified in the **List of signs** parameter. If necessary, SIMULINK resizes the block to show all input ports.

Parameters and Dialog Box

List of signs

A constant or a combination of the symbols + and –. Specifying a constant causes SIMULINK to redraw the block with that number of ports, all with positive polarity. A combination of plus and minus signs specifies the polarity of each port, where the number of ports equals the number of symbols used. All characters other than plus signs, including spaces, are interpreted as minus signs.

Sum

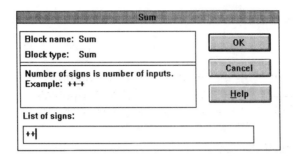

Characteristics

Sample Time		Inherited from driving block
States		0
Direct Feedthrough		Yes

Switch

Switch between two inputs   *Nonlinear library*

Description   The Switch block propagates one of two inputs to its output depending on the value of a third input. If the signal on the second input is greater than or equal to the **Threshold** parameter, the block propagates the first input; otherwise, it propagates the third input.

The width of the output signal is the same as the width of the driving input signal. If all inputs and the **Threshold** parameter are scalars, the output is a scalar. If any input signal or the **Threshold** parameter is a vector, all inputs must be vectors of the same size or, if scalars, are expanded to vectors.

To drive the switch with a logic input (i.e., 0 or 1), you should set the threshold to 0.5.

Parameters and   **Threshold**
Dialog Box   The value of the control (the second input) at which the switch flips to its other state. You can specify this parameter as either a scalar or a vector equal in length to the input vectors. If specified as a scalar, it is expanded to the appropriately sized vector.

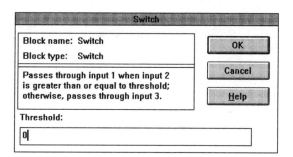

Characteristics   Scalar Expansion   Of inputs and/or the **Threshold** parameter
                      Sample Time   Inherited from driving block
                      States   0
                      Direct Feedthrough   Yes

To File

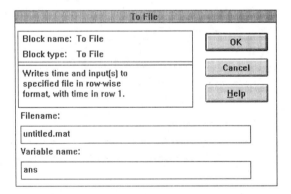

Write data to a file

Sinks library

Description

The To File block writes its input values to a matrix in a **MAT-file**.

The block accepts one input, which can be a scalar or vector. **The block** writes one column for each time step: the first row is **the simulation time** and the remainder of the column is the input data, one **data point for the** scalar input or one point for each element in the input **vector.**

The format used to generate the file is identical to **the format expected by** the From File block. Thus, this output can be used **as input during the** same or a different simulation.

The To File block's icon shows the name of the specified **output file.**

Parameters and Dialog Box

Filename
The name of the MAT-file that holds the matrix. If the **specified file already** exists, the block overwrites its contents.

Variable name
The name of the matrix contained in the named file.

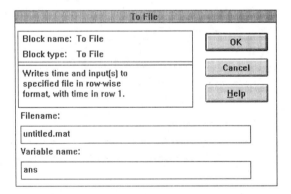

Characteristics

Sample Time	Inherited from driving block
States	0

To Workspace

Write data to a matrix in the workspace   *Sinks library*

Description

The To Workspace block writes its input values to the specified matrix in the workspace.

The block accepts one input, which can be a scalar or vector. By default, the block writes one row for each time step and one data point for the scalar or for each element in the input vector. You can control the amount of data written to the matrix using the **Maximum number of rows** parameter.

If the data is intended to be "played back" in another simulation from a From Workspace block, the first column must contain the simulation time values. You can add a column with time values in two ways:

- By multiplexing the output of a Clock block as the first element of the vector input line of the To Workspace block.

- By specifying time as a return value on the simulation parameters dialog box or from the command line. When the simulation is completed, you can concatenate the time vector (t) to the matrix using a command like this:

```
matrix = [t; matrix];
```

The block displays the name of the matrix to which the data is written.

Parameters and Dialog Box

Variable name
The name of the matrix that holds the data. If the specified matrix already exists in the workspace, the block overwrites the data. The matrix is not available in the workspace until the simulation is terminated.

Maximum number of rows (time steps)
The maximum number of rows (one row per time step) to be collected. You can specify up to two additional optional parameters to specify how often data is collected.

During the simulation, this block writes data to an internal buffer. Then, when the simulation is completed, that data is written to the workspace. You can specify up to three parameters in this field to reduce the effect a prolonged simulation can have on memory usage:

```
[nrows, decimation, sample_time]
```

- The first parameter is the maximum number of rows to be saved. The default is 1000 rows. If the simulation generates more than nrows rows, the block saves only the last nrows rows. If you want to capture all of the data elements, use a number greater than the expected number of steps.

- The second parameter allows you to save data only every nth integration step, where n is the specified decimation.

- The third parameter allows you to specify a **sample time** at which to collect points. This parameter is useful when using a variable step integration in which the interval between each integration step may not be the same.

For example, specifying [100,1,0.5] causes the **To Workspace** block to collect a maximum of 100 points, at time values of 0.5, 1.0, 1.5, ... seconds. Specifying a value of 1 as the second parameter directs the block to collect data at each step. The third parameter specifies that the steps correspond to sample times of 0.5, 1.0, 1.5, etc.

As another example, the entry [100,5,0.5] causes the block to collect up to 100 points, at time values of 2.5, 5.0, 7.5, ... seconds. Specifying 5 as the second parameter directs the block to collect data at every fifth step. The third parameter specifies the sample time, which is the same as in the previous example.

```
                    To Workspace

 Block name:  To Workspace                    OK
 Block type:  To Workspace

 Puts specified matrix in workspace.          Cancel
 Matrix has one column per input,
 one row per simulation step.                 Help

 Variable name:

 yout

 Maximum number of rows (timesteps):

 1000
```

Characteristics

Sample Time	Continuous or discrete
States	0

Transfer Fcn

Implement a linear transfer function   *Linear library*

Description   The Transfer Fcn block implements a transfer function where the input (u) and output (y) can be expressed in transfer function form as the following equation:

$$H(s) = \frac{y(s)}{u(s)} = \frac{num(s)}{den(s)} = \frac{num(1)s^{nn-1} + num(2)s^{nn-2} + \dots + num(nn)}{den(1)s^{nd-1} + den(2)s^{nd-2} + \dots + den(nd)}$$

where nn and nd are the number of numerator and denominator coefficients, respectively. Row vectors *num* and *den* contain the coefficients of the numerator and denominator, respectively, in descending powers of s. These vectors are specified as parameters. The order of the denominator must be greater than or equal to the order of the numerator.

Block input and output are scalar.

Initial conditions are preset to zero. If you need to specify initial conditions, use the State-Space block.

The numerator and denominator are displayed on the Transfer Fcn block icon depending on how they are specified:

- If specified as an expression, a vector, or a variable enclosed in parentheses, the icon shows the transfer function with the specified coefficients and powers of s. If you specify a variable in parentheses, the variable is evaluated. For example, if you specify **Numerator** as [3,2,1] and the **Denominator** as (den) where den is [7,5,3,1], the block would look like this:

$$\frac{3s^2+2s+1}{7s^3+5s^2+3s+1}$$

- If specified as a variable, the icon shows the variable name followed by "(s)". For example, if you specify the **Numerator** as num and the **Denominator** as den, the block would look like this:

$$\frac{num(s)}{den(s)}$$

Parameters and Dialog Box

Numerator

The row vector of numerator coefficients. A matrix with multiple rows can be specified to generate multiple input behavior. The default is [1].

Denominator

The row vector of denominator coefficients. The default is [1 1].

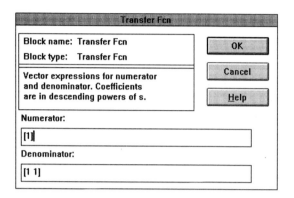

Characteristics

Scalar Expansion	No
Sample Time	Continuous
States	Length of **Denominator** -1
Direct Feedthrough	Yes, if the lengths of the **Numerator** and **Denominator** parameters are equal

Transport Delay

Delay the input by a given amount of time   *Nonlinear library*

Description   The Transport Delay block can be used to simulate a time delay. It delays
the input by a specified amount of time.

At the start of the simulation, the block outputs the **Initial Input** parameter
until the simulation time exceeds the **Time delay** parameter, when the block
begins generating the delayed input. The block stores points from previous
inputs in a circular buffer whose size is defined by the **Initial Buffer size**
parameter.

When outputs are required at times that do not correspond to the times of
the stored values, the block interpolates linearly between points. Therefore, for accurate simulations, you should reduce the maximum step size to
increase the accuracy of the linear interpolation.

The block input can be a scalar or a vector. If a vector, the output is a vector
of the same size and SIMULINK performs scalar expansion on any scalar
parameters.

Using linmod to linearize a model that contains a Transport Delay block
can be troublesome. For more information about ways to avoid the problem,
see "Linearization" in Chapter 4.

This block differs from the Unit Delay block, which delays and holds the
output on sample hits only. The Unit Delay block is equivalent to the
Transport Delay block with a zero-order-hold as its input. The difference
between these two blocks is illustrated with this model:

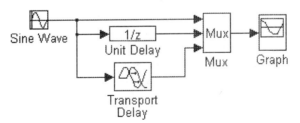

In this model, the Unit Delay is set up with an initial condition of 0 and a
sample time of 1. The Transport Delay block has a time delay of 1 and
initial input of 0. A plot of the output appears below:

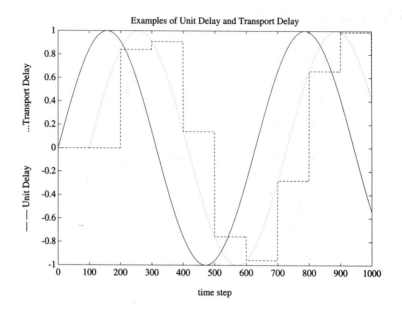

Examples of Unit Delay and Transport Delay

Parameters and Dialog Box

Time delay

The amount of simulation time that the input signal is delayed before propagating the output. If specified as a vector, its size must match that of the block's input. Scalar expansion is performed if necessary.

Initial Input

The output generated by the block between the start of the simulation and the **Time delay**. If specified as a vector, its size must match that of the block's input. Scalar expansion is performed if necessary.

Initial Buffer size

The initial memory allocation for the number of points to store. For long time delays, this block might use a large amount of memory, particularly for a vectorized input. If more buffer storage is required by a simulation, a message is displayed after the simulation suggesting that the buffer size be increased.

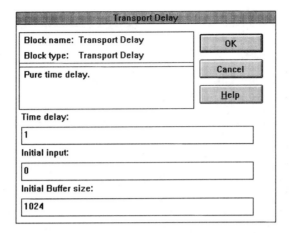

Characteristics

Scalar Expansion	Of parameters
Sample Time	Continuous
States	0
Direct Feedthrough	No

2-D Look-Up Table

Perform piecewise linear mapping of two inputs   *Nonlinear library*

Description

The 2-D Lookup Table block implements piecewise linear mapping of the block inputs into a table defined by the block's parameters.

You define the row and column indices with the **X Index** and **Y Index** parameters, and specify the table as the **Table** parameter. The block produces an output value by comparing the block inputs with X and Y indices:

- If the inputs match X and Y indices, the output is the value at the intersection of those indices.

- If the inputs do not match X and Y indices, it performs linear interpolation between the appropriate X and/or Y indices and generates the appropriate output value from the corresponding table values.

If either or both block inputs are less than the first or greater than the last index, the block extrapolates from the first or last two points.

The 2-D Look-Up Table block supports scalar input and output only.

For a demo of the 2-D Lookup Table block, enter tabdemo in the MATLAB command window.

Parameters and Dialog Box

X Index
The row indices to the table, entered as a row or column vector. The vector values must increase monotonically.

Y Index
The column indices to the table, entered as a row or column vector. The vector values must increase monotonically.

Table
The table of possible output values. The table size must have the dimensions defined by the **X Index** and **Y Index** parameters.

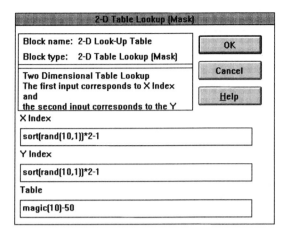

Characteristics

Sample Time	Inherited from driving block
States	0
Direct Feedthrough	Yes

Unit Delay

┤ 1/z ├

Delay a signal one sample period   *Discrete library*

Description   The Unit Delay block delays and holds its input signal by one sampling interval. If the input to the block is a vector, all elements of the vector are delayed by the same sample delay. This block is equivalent to the z^{-1} discrete-time operator.

If an undelayed sample and hold function is desired, use a Zero-Order Hold block, or if a delay of greater than one unit is desired, use a Discrete Transfer Fcn block. (See the description of the Transport Delay block for an example that uses the Unit Delay block with an initial condition of 0 and a sample time of 1.)

Parameters and   **Sample time**
Dialog Box   The time interval between samples. The sample time is specified as a scalar or a two-element vector. The first element is the sample time; the second element, if present, is the offset time. The offset time allows the sample hit to be offset from the end of the sample period. A positive offset specifies a lag; a negative offset specifies a lead for each sample hit.

Initial condition
The block output for the first simulation period, during which the output of the Unit Delay block is undefined. Careful selection of this parameter can minimize unwanted output behavior during this time. The default is 0.

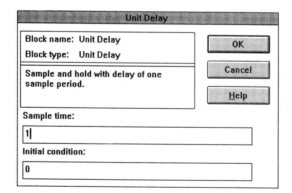

Characteristics   Scalar Expansion   Of the **Initial condition** parameter
Sample Time   Discrete
States   Inherited from driving block or parameters
Direct Feedthrough   No

Variable Transport Delay

Delay the input by a variable amount of time

Nonlinear library

Description

The Variable Transport Delay block can be used to simulate a variable time delay. The block might be used to model a system with a pipe where the speed of a motor pumping fluid in the pipe is variable.

The block accepts two inputs: the first input is the signal that passes through the block; the second input is the time delay. During the simulation the block stores time and input value pairs in an internal buffer. At the start of the simulation, the block outputs the **Initial Input** parameter until the simulation time exceeds the time delay input. At each simulation step, the block outputs the signal at the time that corresponds to the current simulation time minus the delay time.

When outputs are required at times that do not correspond to the times of the stored values, the block interpolates linearly between points. The block also extrapolates for times before the start of the simulation.

The block inputs can be scalars or vectors. If vectors, they must be the same size. The output is a scalar unless either input is a vector. SIMULINK performs scalar expansion on any scalar inputs and parameters.

This block produces more accurate results when you use a smaller maximum step size or a fixed step size (where the minimum and maximum step size are the same). If the time delay goes negative, future points are predicted by linearly extrapolating the last two input points.

Parameters and Dialog Box

Maximum delay
The maximum value of the time delay input.

Initial Input
The output generated by the block until the simulation time first exceeds the time delay input.

Buffer size
The number of points the block can store. For long delays, this block might use a large amount of memory, particularly for a vectorized input.

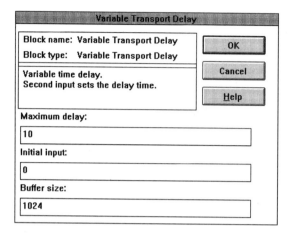

Characteristics   Sample Time   Continuous
States   0
Direct Feedthrough   Yes

XY Graph Scope

Display X-Y plot of signals using MATLAB figure window　　　　　*Sinks library*

Description

The XY Graph Scope block displays an X-Y plot of its inputs in a MATLAB figure window. The block has two scalar inputs. The block plots data in the first input (the *x* direction) against data in the second input (the *y* direction). This block is useful for examining limit cycles and other two-state data. Data outside the specified range is not displayed.

For a demo that illustrates the use of the XY Graph Scope block, enter lorenzs in the command window.

Parameters and Dialog Box

x-min
The minimum *x*-axis value. The default is -10.

x-max
The maximum *x*-axis value. The default is 10.

y-min
The minimum *y*-axis value. The default is -10.

y-max
The maximum *y*-axis value. The default is 10.

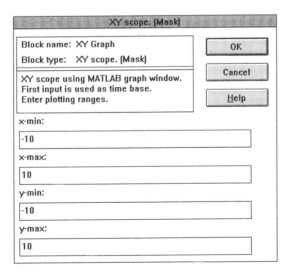

Characteristics　　Sample Time　　　　　Inherited from driving block
　　　　　　　　　　　States　　　　　　　　2 discrete

Zero-Order Hold

Zero-order hold of one sample period   *Discrete library*

Description   The Zero-Order Hold block implements a sample-and-hold function operating at the specified sampling rate. The block accepts one input and generates one output, both of which can be scalar or vector.

This block provides a mechanism for discretizing one or more signals. You can use it in instances where you need to model sampling without requiring one of the other more complex discrete function blocks. For example, it could be used in conjunction with a Gain block to model an A/D converter with an input amplifier.

Parameters and Dialog Box

Sample time

The time interval between samples. The sample time is specified as a scalar or a two-element vector. The first element is the sample time; the second element, if present, is the offset time. The offset time allows the sample hit to be offset from the end of the sample period. A positive offset specifies a lag; a negative offset specifies a lead for each sample hit.

```
                        Zero-Order Hold
 ┌────────────────────────────────────────┐
 │ Block name: Zero-Order Hold    ┌──────┐ │
 │ Block type:  Zero-Order Hold   │  OK  │ │
 │ ┌─────────────────────────┐    └──────┘ │
 │ │ Zero-order hold of one  │   ┌────────┐ │
 │ │ sample period.          │   │ Cancel │ │
 │ │                         │   └────────┘ │
 │ │                         │   ┌────────┐ │
 │ └─────────────────────────┘   │  Help  │ │
 │ Sample time:                  └────────┘ │
 │ ┌─────────────────────────────────────┐ │
 │ │ 1│                                   │ │
 │ └─────────────────────────────────────┘ │
 └────────────────────────────────────────┘
```

Characteristics   Sample Time   Discrete
                       States   0
                       Direct Feedthrough   Yes

$$\frac{(s-1)}{s(s+1)}$$

Zero-Pole

Implement a transfer function specified in terms of poles and zeros   *Linear library*

Description   The Zero-Pole block implements a system with the specified zeros, poles, and gain in terms of the Laplace operator s.

A transfer function can be expressed in factored or zero-pole-gain form, which, for a single-input single-output system in MATLAB, is:

$$H(s) = K\frac{Z(s)}{P(s)} = K\frac{(s-Z(1))(s-Z(2))\dots(s-Z(n))}{(s-P(1))(s-P(2))\dots(s-P(n))}$$

where Z represents the zeros vector, P represents the poles vector, and K represents the scalar gain.

The block accepts one scalar input and generates one scalar output.

The Zero-Pole block displays the transfer function in its icon depending on how the parameters are specified:

- If specified as an expression, a vector, or a variable enclosed in parentheses, the icon shows the transfer function with the specified zeros, poles, and gain. If you specify a variable in parentheses, the variable is evaluated. For example, if you specify the **Zeros** as [3,2,1], the **Poles** as (poles) (where poles is defined in the workspace as [7,5,3,1]), and the **Gain** as gain, the icon would look like this:

$$\frac{gain(s\text{-}3)(s\text{-}2)(s\text{-}1)}{(s\text{-}7)(s\text{-}5)(s\text{-}3)(s\text{-}1)}$$

- If specified as a variable, the icon shows the variable name followed by "(s)". For example, if you specify the **Zeros** as zeros, the **Poles** as poles, and the **Gain** as gain, the icon would look like this:

$$\frac{gain^{*}zeros(s)}{poles(s)}$$

Parameters and Dialog Box   **Zeros**
The vector of zeros. The default is [1].

Poles
The vector of poles. The default is [0; -1].

Gain

The scalar gain, entered as a number or variable. The default is [1].

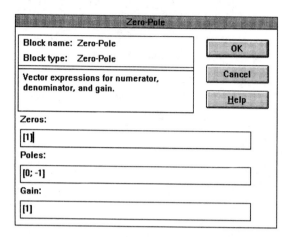

Characteristics

Sample Time	Continuous
States	Variable
Direct Feedthrough	Yes, if the lengths of the **Poles** and **Zeros** parameters are equal

7

Analysis Commands

This chapter provides detailed reference information about commands used to analyze simulations. It includes these categories of commands:

Integration algorithms:

- linsim
- rk23 (Runge-Kutta 23)
- rk45 (Runge-Kutta 45)
- adams
- gear
- euler

Linearization analysis:

- linmod – Extracts the linear state-space model of a system around an operating point.
- dlinmod – Extracts the linear state-space discrete-time model of a system around an operating point.
- linmod2 – An advanced form of linearization.

Trim analysis:

- trim – Finds steady state parameters that satisfy input, output, and state conditions.

Integration Methods

Integrate a system of ordinary differential equations

Syntax

[t,x,y] = *method*('*model*', tfinal)

[t,x,y] = *method*('*model*', tfinal, x0)

[t,x,y] = *method*('*model*', tfinal, x0, options)

[t,x,y] = *method*('*model*', tfinal, x0, options, ut)

method('*model*', t)

Arguments

t,x,y
Returned values of time (t), state (x), and output (y). If the left-hand arguments are not specified and the model has outputs, they are displayed in graphical form; otherwise, state trajectories are plotted.

method
Integration method: linsim, rk23, rk45, adams, gear, or euler.

model
Model name, enclosed in single quotes.

tfinal
Simulation start and stop time. If specified as a scalar, tfinal is the stop time and the start time is 0. If specified as a two-element vector, [tstart tfinal], it defines the start and stop times.

x0
Initial conditions vector. If specified, they override initial conditions set in the blocks, unless x0 is an empty matrix.

options
A six-element optional vector of simulation parameters. Default values are used if the options vector is not specified, is empty, or contains zeros.

options(1)	Tolerance or relative error (default 1e-3)
options(2)	Minimum step size (default tfinal/2000)
options(3)	Maximum step size (default tfinal/50)
options(4)	A value of 1 selects Adams/Gear, which chooses the appropriate method (either Adams or Gear), depending on the model stiffness.
options(5)	A nonzero value displays a warning message when the minimum step size is reached, indicating that the error tolerance is not being met. This can occur when there are discontinuities in the system. The default is to suppress warning messages.
options(6)	Plot parameter (1 is plot on, 2 is plot off)
	The default is to set plotting on when no left-hand arguments are supplied.

ut   External inputs. ut can be either a string or a table of values.

If specified as a string, MATLAB evaluates its contents and uses the result as the external input to the system. The string can be an expression that contains workspace variables. For example, specifying 'sin(t)' inputs, at each time step, *sin(t)*.

If specified as a matrix, the first column must be a vector of times in ascending order. The last n columns must be the corresponding input values for the n inputs. SIMULINK linearly interpolates between time/input values when necessary. For example, these statements provide input values at the computed values of t:

```
t = 0:0.1:10;
u = [cos(t), sin(t), tan(t)];
ut = [t, u];
rk45(model, t, [], [0,min,max], ut];
```

Description

With three left-hand arguments, the integration function returns the simulation time points t, the state trajectories x, and output trajectories y.

Without left-hand arguments, the statement integrates the system of ordinary differential equations described in *model* between 0 and tfinal seconds. If the model has outputs, they are displayed in graphical form; otherwise, state trajectories are plotted.

Step Size Control

All the supplied integration functions are variable step methods with different algorithms. The step size is continually adjusted to meet the relative error criterion. The step size indicates the minimum distance between points generated for the output trajectories.

The step size for the output and state trajectories is maintained in the range options(2) ≤ step size ≤ options(3). All algorithms, other than gear and adams, can be converted to fixed-step methods by setting the minimum step size, options(2), equal to the maximum step size, options(3).

linsim and euler are single-step methods that generate a new output point every time step. rk23 and rk45 are Runge-Kutta methods that take steps between the points generated for the output trajectories.

• rk23 is a third order method, which uses a second order method for step-size control. It takes three steps to generate one output point. The minimum step size is options(2)/2.

• rk45 is a fifth order method, which uses a fourth order method for step-size control. It takes six unevenly spaced points between the output points. The minimum step size is options(2)/13.

The adams and gear routines are predictor-corrector methods, which take a variable number of points to generate one output point.

All the integration algorithms (except euler) reduce the step size when the predicted error is calculated to be greater than the relative error. The step size is never reduced below options(2). Therefore, it is possible to obtain inaccurate results if either the relative error, options(1), or the minimum step size, options(2), is too large.

Examples

This command describes the Van der Pol model. The sizes vector displays model characteristics (comments indicate what each vector element means), the x0 vector displays the block initial conditions, and the str vector indicates the state (and initial condition) ordering:

```
[sizes,x0,str] = vdp)[], [], [], 0)
sizes = 2    number of continuous states
        0    number of discrete states
        0    number of outputs
        0    number of inputs
        0    unused element
        0    no direct feedthrough
        1    number of sample times

x0 =    0.25
        0.25

str =   /vdp/int x2
        /vdp int x1
```

To confirm these results, enter vdp in the command window. Block names in the model are hidden. To display them, select the Integrator blocks, then choose **Displayed** on the **Title** option on the **Style** menu.

To start the simulation from a command, plotting states vs. time and using the block initial conditions, use this command:

```
rk45('vdp', 10, [], [1e-3 .01 .1])
```

The third argument is specified as an empty matrix, which causes the integrator to use the initial conditions specified in the blocks.

To override the block initial conditions, use this command:

```
rk45('vdp', 10, [2.5 2.5], [1e-3 .01 .1])
```

This command uses initial conditions of 2.5 for the Integrator blocks.

References

[1] Forsythe, G. F., M.A. Malcolm, C.B. Moler, *Computer Methods for Mathematical Computations*, Prentice Hall, 1977.

[2] Kahaner, D., C.B. Moler, S. Nash, *Numerical Methods and Software*, Prentice Hall, 1989.

Linearization Analysis

Extract the linear state-space model of a system around an operating point

Syntax   [A,B,C,D] = *linfun*('model')

[A,B,C,D] = *linfun*('model', x, u)

[A,B,C,D] = *linfun*('model', x, u, pert)

[A,B,C,D] = *linfun*('model', x, u, pert, xpert, upert)

Arguments

linfun	linmod, dlinmod, or linmod2.
model	The name of the system from which the linear model is to be extracted.
x and u	The state and the input vectors. If specified, they set the operating point at which the linear model is to be extracted.
pert	Optional scalar perturbation factor used for both x and u. If not specified, a default value of 1e-5 is used.

xpert and upert
Optional vectors that can explicitly set perturbation levels for individual states and inputs. If specified, the pert argument is ignored.

the i-th state x is perturbed to x(i) + xpert(i)

the j-th input u is perturbed to u(j) + upert(j)

Description   linmod obtains linear models from systems of ordinary differential equations described as SIMULINK models. linmod returns the linear model in state space-form, *A*, *B*, *C*, *D*, which describes the linearized input-output relationship:

$$\dot{x} = Ax + Bu$$
$$y = Cx + Du$$

Inputs and outputs are denoted in SIMULINK block diagrams using Inport and Outport blocks.

[A,B,C,D] = linmod('model') obtains the linearized model of model around an operating point with the state variables x and the input u set to zero.

linmod perturbs the states around the operating point to determine the rate of change in the state derivatives and outputs (Jacobians). This result is used to calculate the state-space matrices. Each state x(i) is perturbed to

$$x(i) + \Delta(i)$$

where

$$\Delta(i) = \delta(1 + |x(i)|)$$

Likewise the j-th input is perturbed to

$$u(j) + \Delta(j)$$

where

$$\Delta(j) = \delta(1 + |u(j)|)$$

Discrete-Time System Linearization

The function dlinmod can linearize discrete, multirate, and hybrid continuous and discrete systems at any given sampling time. Use the same calling syntax for dlinmod as for linmod, but insert the sample time at which to perform the linearization as the second argument. For example:

```
[Ad,Bd,Cd,Dd] = dlinmod('model', Ts, x, u);
```

produces a discrete state-space model at the sampling time Ts and the operating point given by the state vector x and input vector u. To obtain a continuous model approximation of a discrete system, set Ts to 0.

For systems composed of linear, multirate, discrete and continuous blocks, dlinmod produces linear models that have identical frequency and time responses (for constant inputs) at the converted sampling time Ts, provided that:

• Ts is an integer multiple of all the sampling times in the system.

• Ts is not less than the slowest sample time in the system.

• The system is stable.

It is possible for valid linear models to be obtained when these conditions are not met.

Computing the eigenvalues of the linearized matrix Ad provides an indication of the stability of the system; therefore, if Ts>0 and the eigenvalues are within the unit circle, determined by this statement, the system is stable.

```
all(abs(eig(Ad))) < 1
```

Likewise, the system is stable if Ts=0 and the eigenvalues are in the left half plane, as determined by this statement:

```
all(real(eig(Ad))) < 0
```

When the system is unstable and the sample time is not an integer multiple of the other sampling times, dlinmod may produce Ad and Bd matrices, which may be complex. The eigenvalues of the Ad matrix in this case still, however, provide a good indication of stability.

dlinmod can be used to convert the sample times of a system to other values or to convert a linear discrete system to a continuous system or vice versa.

The frequency response of a continuous system can be found by using the bode command.

An Advanced Form of Linearization

The linmod2 routine provides an advanced form of linearization. This routine takes longer to run than linmod but may produce more accurate results.

The calling syntax for linmod2 is similar to that used for linmod but functions differently. For instance, linmod2('model',x,u) produces a linear model as does linmod; however, the perturbation levels for each state-space matrix element are set individually to attempt to minimize errors associated with roundoff and truncation errors.

linmod2 tries to balance the trade-off that occurs between roundoff error (caused by small perturbation levels, which cause errors associated with finite precision mathematics) and truncation error (caused by large perturbation levels, which invalidate the piecewise linear approximation).

With the form [A,B,C,D] = linmod2('model',x,u,pert), the variable pert indicates the lowest level of perturbation that can be used; the default is 1e-8. linmod2 has the advantage that it can detect discontinuities and produce warning messages, such as the following:

```
Warning: discontinuity detected at A(2,3)
```

When such a warning occurs, try a different operating point at which to obtain the linear model.

With the form

```
[A,B,C,D] = linmod2('model',x,u,pert,Apert,Bpert,Cpert,Dpert)
```

the variables Apert, Bpert, Cpert, and Dpert are matrices used to set the perturbation levels for each state and input combination; therefore, the ij-th element of xpert is the perturbation level associated with obtaining the ij-th element of the A matrix. Default perturbation sizes are returned using

```
[A,B,C,D,Apert,Bpert,Cpert,Dpert] = linmod2('model', x, u);
```

Notes
By default, the system time is set to zero. For systems that are dependent on time, the variable `pert` can be set to a two-element vector, where the second element is used to set the value of `t` at which to obtain the linear model.

When the model being linearized is itself a linear model, the problem of truncation error no longer exists; therefore, the perturbation levels can be set to whatever value is desired. A relatively high value is generally preferable, since this tends to reduce roundoff error. The operating point used does not affect the linear model obtained.

The ordering of the states from the nonlinear model to the linear model is maintained. For SIMULINK systems, a string variable that contains the block name associated with each state can be obtained using

```
[sizes,x0,xstring] = model
```

where `xstring` is a vector of strings whose `i`-th row is the block name associated with the `i`-th state. Inputs and outputs are numbered sequentially on the diagram.

For single-input multi-output systems, you can convert to transfer function form using the routine `ss2tf` or to zero-pole form using `ss2zp`.

Linearizing a model that contains Derivative or Transport Delay blocks can be troublesome. For more information, see "Linearization" in Chapter 4.

Trim Analysis

Determine steady state parameters that satisfy input, output, and state conditions

Syntax

```
[x,u,y,dx] = trim('model')

[x,u,y,dx] = trim('model',x0,u0,y0)

[x,u,y,dx] = trim('model',x0,u0,y0,ix,iu,iy)

[x,u,y,dx] = trim('model',x0,u0,y0,ix,iu,iy,dx0,idx)

[x,u,y,dx] = trim('model',x0,u0,y0,ix,iu,iy,dx0,idx,options)

[x,u,y,dx] = trim('model',x0,u0,y0,ix,iu,iy,dx0,idx,options,t)

[x,u,y,dx,options] = trim('model',...)

[x,u,y,dx] = trim2('model',...)

[x,u,y,dx] = trim3('model',...)

[x,u,y,dx] = trim4('model',...)
```

Description

trim attempts to find values for the inputs u and states x that set the state derivatives to zero. Such a point is known as an equilibrium point, which occurs when the system is in steady state.

Since the problem is usually not unique, specific values of the state x, the input u, and the outputs y can often be fixed.

[x,u,y] = trim('model') tries to find an equilibrium point such that the maximum absolute value of [x;u;y] is minimized.

[x,u,y] = trim('model',x0,u0,y0) specifies initial starting guesses for x, u, and y, respectively. In this case, the maximum value of abs([x–x0; u–u0; y–y0]) is minimized.

Individual elements of x, u, and y can be fixed using the syntax

```
trim('model', x0, u0, y0, ix, iu, iy)
```

The integer vectors ix, iu, and iy are used to single out elements in x0, u0, and y0 to be fixed. Since there is no guarantee of a solution point, the method finds steady state values that minimize the maximum value of

```
abs([x(ix)–x0(ix); u(iu)–u0(iu); y(iy)–y0(iy)])
```

trim uses a constrained optimization method, which restricts the state derivatives to be zero, and solves a minimax problem formed from the desired values for x, u, and y. It is possible that no feasible solution exists to this problem, in which case `trim` minimizes the worst case deviation from zero of the state derivatives.

To fix the derivatives to nonzero values use

```
[x,u,y,dx] = trim('model', x0, u0, y0, ix, iu, iy, dx0, idx)
```

where `dx0` represents the desired derivative values, and `idx` indexes the elements in `dx` to be fixed.

The `trim` command takes an optional argument, `options`, used with optimization routines. This argument is beyond the scope of the Student Edition.

Examples

Consider a linear state-space model

$$\dot{x} = Ax + Bu$$
$$y = Cx + Du$$

The A, B, C, and D matrices are as follows in a system called `'model'`:

```
A = [−0.09  −0.01;  1    0];
B = [ 0     −7;     0   −2];
C = [ 0      2;     1   −5];
D = [−3      0;     1    0];
```

Example 1

To find an equilibrium point use

```
[x,u,y,dx,options] = trim('model')

x =
      0
      0
u =
      0
y =
      0
      0
dx =
      0
      0
```

The number of iterations taken is

```
options(10)
ans =
        7
```

Example 2

To find an equilibrium point near x = [1;1], u = [1;1] enter

```
x0 = [1;1];
u0 = [1;1];
[x,u,y,dx,options] = trim('model', x0, u0);

x =
        1.0e-11 *
      -0.1167
      -0.1167
u =
        0.3333
        0.0000
y =
      -1.0000
        0.3333
dx =
        1.0e-11 *
        0.4214
        0.0003
```

The number of iterations taken is

```
options(10)
ans =
       25
```

Example 3

To find an equilibrium point with the outputs fixed to 1, use

```
y = [1;1];
iy = [1;2];
[x,u,y,dx] = trim('model', [], [], y, [], [], iy)

x =
      0.0009
     -0.3075
u =
     -0.5383
      0.0004
y =
      1.0000
      1.0000
dx =
      1.0e-16 *
     -0.0173
      0.2396
```

Example 4

To find an equilibrium point with the outputs fixed to 1 and the second derivatives set to 0 and 1, use

```
y = [1;1];
iy = [1;2];
dx = [0;1];
idx = [1;2];
[x,u,y,dx,options] = trim('model',[],[],y,[],[],iy,dx,idx)

x =
      0.9752
     -0.0827
u =
     -0.3884
     -0.0124
y =
      1.0000
      1.0000
dx =
      0.0000
      1.0000
```

The number of iterations taken is

```
options(10)
ans =
        13
```

Limitations

When a steady state solution is found, better values for x, u, and y may exist because there is no guarantee of global solutions unless the optimization problem is univariate (i.e., has a single minimum). Thus, it is important to try a number of starting guesses for x, u, and y if you seek global solutions. trim does not work well when the system has discontinuities.

Algorithm

trim uses a constrained optimization routine, which restricts the state derivatives to zero, and solves a minimax problem formed from the desired values for x, u, and y. The underlying method is Sequential Quadratic Programming.

A

Block Characteristics Tables

This appendix provides a tabular summary of the characteristics of the blocks in all block libraries except the Extras library. This information is summarized from the individual block reference pages in Chapter 6.

Block libraries are arranged in alphabetical order. Blocks within library tables are also arranged alphabetically.

The **Inputs**, **Outputs**, or **Inputs/Outputs** column indicates how many input and/or output ports a block supports.

The **Vectorized** column indicates whether the block accepts vector inputs and/ or generates vector outputs. For more information, see "Vectorization of Blocks" in Chapter 3.

The **Input Width** and **Output Width** columns indicate how the widths of inputs or outputs are determined. "Inherited" means that the width is determined from the driving block. "Explicit" means that the width is specified on the block's dialog box.

The **Scalar Expansion** column indicates whether SIMULINK performs scalar expansion of inputs and/or parameters. For more information, see "Scalar Expansion of Inputs and Parameters" in Chapter 3.

The **Sample Time** column indicates whether the block is Discrete, Continuous, or whether its sample time is inherited by the driving block.

The **States** column indicates the number of states. States typically depend on block parameters.

The **Direct Feedthrough** column indicates whether the block has direct feedthrough and, therefore, can be part of an algebraic loop. For more information, see "Algebraic Loops" in Chapter 4.

Connections Library Block Characteristics

Block Name	Inputs/ Outputs	Vectorized	Input Width	Scalar Expansion	Sample Time	States	Direct Feedthrough
Demux	1/n	Yes/Yes	Explicit	N/A	Inherited	0	Yes
Import	–/1	–/Yes	N/A	N/A	Top level: N/A; Subsystems: inherited	0	Yes in subsystems
Mux	n/1	Yes/Yes	Explicit	N/A	Inherited	0	Yes
Outport	1/–	Yes/–	N/A	N/A	Top level: N/A; Subsystems: inherited	0	Yes in subsystems
Subsystem	n/n	Yes/Yes	Variable	Variable	Variable	Variable	Variable

Discrete Library Block Characteristics

Block Name	Inputs/ Outputs	Vectorized	Input Width	Scalar Expansion	Sample Time	States	Direct Feedthrough
Discrete State-Space	1/1	Yes/Yes	B and D matrices	N/A	Discrete	Variable, size of A	If D ≠ 0
Discrete-Time Int.	1/1	Yes/Yes	Inherited	Of I.C.	Discrete	Variable	No
Discrete-Time Limited Integrator	1/1	Yes/Yes	Inherited	Of I.C. and bounds	Discrete	Inherited	No
Discrete Transfer Fcn	1/1	No/No	N/A	N/A	Discrete	Length of den - 1	If num and den lengths equal
Discrete Zero-Pole	1/1	No/No	N/A	N/A	Discrete	Length of Poles	If # of poles = # of zeros
Filter	1/1	No/No	N/A	N/A	Discrete	Length of den - 1	If num and den lengths equal
First-Order Hold	1/1	Yes/Yes	Inherited	N/A	Continuous	1 cont, 1 disc per input element	No
Unit Delay	1/1	Yes/Yes	Inherited	Of I.C.	Discrete	Inherited or parameters	No
Zero-Order Hold	1/1	Yes/Yes	Inherited	N/A	Discrete	0	Yes

Linear Library Block Characteristics

Block Name	Inputs/Outputs	Vectorized	Input Width	Scalar Expansion	Sample Time	States	Direct Feedthrough
Derivative	1/1	Yes/Yes	Inherited	N/A	Continuous	0	Yes
Gain	1/1	Yes/Yes	Inherited or Gain	Of Gain	Inherited	0	Yes
Inner Product	2/1	Yes/No	Inherited	Of input	Inherited	0	Yes
Integrator	1/1	Yes/Yes	Inherited or I.C.	Of I.C.	Continuous	# inputs	No
Matrix Gain	1/1	Yes/Yes	Size of Gain matrix	No	Inherited	0	Yes
Slider Gain	1/1	Yes/Yes	Inherited or gain	Of gain	Inherited	0	Yes
State-Space	1/1	Yes/Yes	B and C matrices	N/A	Continuous	Variable, size of A	If $D \neq 0$
Sum	n/1	Yes/Yes	Inherited	Inputs	Inherited	0	Yes
Transfer Fcn	1/1	No/No	N/A	N/A	Continuous	Length of den - 1	If num and den lengths equal
Zero-Pole	1/1	No/No	N/A	N/A	Continuous	Variable	If poles and zeros lengths equal

Nonlinear Library Block Characteristics

Block Name	Inputs/Outputs	Vectorized	Input Width	Scalar Expansion	Sample Time	States	Direct Feedthrough
Abs	1/1	Yes/Yes	Inherited	N/A	Inherited	0	Yes
Backlash	1/1	Yes/Yes	Inherited or parameters	Parameters	Inherited	0	Yes
Combinatorial Logic	1/1	Yes/Yes	$\log_2$ of length of logic table	No	Inherited	0	Yes
Coulombic Friction	1/1	Yes/Yes	Inherited	No	Inherited	0	Yes

Nonlinear Library Block Characteristics

Block Name	Inputs/ Outputs	Vectorized	Input Width	Scalar Expansion	Sample Time	States	Direct Feedthrough
Dead Zone	1/1	Yes/Yes	Inherited or parameters	Parameters	Inherited	0	Yes
Fcn	1/1	Yes/No	Inherited	No	Inherited	0	Yes
Limited Integrator	1/1	Yes/Yes	Inherited or parameters	Parameters	Continuous	Inherited or parameters	No
Logical Operator	n/1	Yes/Yes	Inherited	Inputs	Inherited	0	Yes
Look-Up Table	1/1	Yes/Yes	Inherited	Of lookup table	Inherited	0	Yes
MATLAB Fcn	1/1	Yes/Yes	Inherited	N/A	Inherited	0	Yes
Memory	1/1	Yes/Yes	Inherited	Of I.C.	Continuous	0	Yes
Product	n/1	Yes/Yes	Inherited	Inputs	Inherited	0	Yes
Quantizer	1/1	Yes/Yes	Inherited	Parameters	Inherited	0	Yes
Rate Limiter	1/1	Yes/Yes	Inherited or parameters	Parameters	Inherited	0	Yes
Relational Operator	2/1	Yes/Yes	Inherited	Inputs	Inherited	0	Yes
Relay	1/1	Yes/Yes	Inherited or parameters	Parameters	Inherited	0	Yes
Reset Integrator	3/1	Yes/Yes	Inherited or # of I.C.	Inputs and I.C.	Continuous	Inherited or I.C.	No
Saturation	1/1	Yes/Yes	Inherited	Parameters	Inherited	0	Yes
S-Function	1/1	Yes/Yes	Variable	Variable	Variable	Variable	Variable
Sign	1/1	Yes/Yes	Inherited	N/A	Inherited	0	Yes
Switch	3/1	Yes/Yes	Inherited or threshold	Inputs and/ or threshold	Inherited	0	Yes
Transport Delay	1/1	Yes/Yes	Inherited or delay times	Parameters	Continuous	0	No
2-D Look-Up Table	2/1	No/No	N/A	No	Inherited	0	Yes
Variable Transport Delay	2/1	Yes/Yes	Inherited	Inputs and parameters	Continuous	0	Yes

Sinks Library Block Characteristics

Block Name	Inputs	Vectorized	Input Width	Scalar Expansion	Sample Time	States	Direct Feedthrough
Auto-Scale Graph Scope	1	Yes	Inherited	N/A	Inherited	9 discrete	N/A
Graph Scope	1	Yes	Inherited	N/A	Inherited	4 discrete	N/A
Hit Crossing	1	Yes	Inherited	Yes	Continuous	Inherited	N/A
Scope	1	Yes	Inherited	N/A	Inherited	0	N/A
Stop Simulation	1	Yes	Inherited	N/A	Inherited	0	N/A
To File	1	Yes	Inherited	N/A	Inherited	0	N/A
To Workspace	1	Yes	Inherited	N/A	Continuous or Discrete	0	N/A
XY Graph Scope	2	No	N/A	N/A	Inherited	2 discrete	N/A

Sources Library Block Characteristics

Block Name	Outputs	Vectorized	Output Width	Scalar Expansion	Sample Time	States	Direct Feedthrough
Band-Limited White Noise	1	Yes	N/A	N/A	Discrete	0	N/A
Chirp Signal	1	No	N/A	N/A	Continuous	0	N/A
Clock	1	No	N/A	N/A	Continuous	0	N/A
Constant	1	Yes	Length of parameter	No	Constant	0	N/A
Digital Clock	1	No	N/A	N/A	Discrete	0	N/A
From File	1	Yes	# variables in file	N/A	Inherited	0	N/A
From Workspace	1	Yes	# variable columns	N/A	Inherited	0	N/A
Pulse Generator	1	No	N/A	N/A	Continuous	Yes	N/A
Random Number	1	Yes	Length of parameter	Parameters	Inherited	0	N/A

Sources Library Block Characteristics

Block Name	Outputs	Vectorized	Output Width	Scalar Expansion	Sample Time	States	Direct Feedthrough
Repeating Sequence	1	No	N/A	N/A	Continuous	0	N/A
Signal Generator	1	No	N/A	N/A	Inherited	0	N/A
Sine Wave	1	Yes	Length of parameter	Parameters	Continuous or Discrete	0	N/A
Step Input	1	Yes	Length of parameters	Parameters	Inherited	0	N/A

The Extras Block Library

This appendix describes the blocks contained in these Extras library sublibraries:

- Conversion
- Flip-Flops
- PID Controllers
- Analyzers
- Filters

Conversion Blocks

The Conversion blocks perform several commonly used coordinate transformations.

- Polar to Cartesian coordinate transformation
- Cartesian to polar coordinate transformation
- Spherical to Cartesian coordinate transformation
- Cartesian to spherical coordinate transformation

These blocks have no parameters. You can learn more about the equations that define the transformations by unmasking the blocks and examining the underlying function blocks.

Flip-Flops

This sublibrary contains a collection of flip-flops and a clock that has been optimized to generate sharp rising and falling edges, which is important for accurate operation of the flip-flops.

Latch

This is a standard set-reset latch. It has two inputs, S (Set) and R (Reset), and two outputs, 1 (uncomplemented) and 0 (complemented). When a TRUE value is applied to the S input, the uncomplemented output becomes one, and the complemented output becomes zero. It remains one until a TRUE value is applied to the R input. This forces the uncomplemented output to zero. A FALSE value on either input has no effect on the output of the latch. If both S and R are TRUE at the same time, the latch is put into an undefined state. The latch is initially in the reset state. The block accepts the initial state as its parameter.

D Flip-Flop

The D (Delay) flip-flop has two inputs, D and clock, and two outputs, uncomplemented and complemented. Its output can change only when the clock input is TRUE. During this time, the output is zero if the D input is FALSE and one if the D input is TRUE. When the clock input changes to FALSE, the D flip-flop latches the value of the D input at the trailing edge of the clock pulse. It maintains this value until the clock input goes TRUE again. The block accepts the initial state as its parameter.

SR Flip-Flop

The SR flip-flop is a clocked latch. Its operation is the same as the latch, except that it is only susceptible to input changes when the clock input is TRUE. When the clock is FALSE, the SR flip-flop maintains the output at the value that it had at the trailing edge of the clock pulse. The block accepts the initial state as its parameter.

JK Flip-Flop

The JK flip-flop has three inputs, J, K, and clock, and two outputs, uncomplemented and complemented. If the output is currently zero, a TRUE value on the J input causes the output to change to one when the clock value is TRUE. The K value has no effect on the output in this case. If the output is currently one, a TRUE value on the K input causes the output to change to zero when the clock input is TRUE. The J input has no effect on the output in this case. The block accepts the initial state as its parameter.

Note that, unlike the latch or the SR flip-flop, both J and K can be TRUE at the same time. This condition toggles the output value; i.e., if the output is currently one, it changes to zero, and if the output is zero, it changes to one.

Clock

This is a digital clock for logic systems. It outputs a square wave with the period specified in the block's dialog box. The output values are zero for low and one for high. When using the various logic blocks, it is important that the period of the clock be much greater than the maximum step size of the integration method used. Therefore, it may be necessary to scale the **Period** parameter value appropriately. For example, if the system's clock period is 1 μsec, enter 1 for the clock period and use units of μsec rather than entering 0.000001 for the clock period with units of seconds.

PID Controllers

The PID Controller block uses proportional, integral, and derivative control in the form P + I/s + Ds. You can see how this block is created by unmasking it.

You can learn more about approaches to PID controller tuning in the following references:

- Åström, K. J. and B. Wittenmark, *Computer Controlled Systems*, 2nd edition, Prentice Hall, 1990, p. 221-235.

- Åström, K. J. and T. Hagglund, *Automatic Tuning of PID Regulators*, Instrument Society of America, Research Triangle Park, N.C.

An approach to tuning a PID controller using the Optimization Toolbox can be found in:

• Grace, A. C. W., "SIMULAB, An Interactive Environment for Simulation and Control," *Proceedings of the American Control Conference*, Boston, July, 1991.

Analyzers

This sublibrary contains a collection of display devices.

Power Spectral Density

The Power Spectral Density block displays the power spectral density of a specified number of input data points. The block's dialog box allows you to specify these parameters:

- **Length of buffer** – The number of input data points over which the power spectral density is calculated.

- **Number of points for fft** – The number of points used to calculate the FFT should normally be set to the length of the buffer and, for efficiency, should be a power of 2. Setting it to more than the number of points in the buffer pads the FFT with zeros and has the effect of giving a smoother graph with more frequency points. Choosing a value with fewer points than the number of points in the buffer produces a coarser graph, but one in which the frequency points are averaged.

- **Plot after how many points** – This value determines how often the graph is redrawn and normally should be set to the length of the buffer. To see the graph appear more often, you can set this value to a lower number. Note that in all cases the power spectral density is calculated using the number of points specified with the **Length of buffer** parameter; the value specified with this parameter determines when the data is replotted.

- **Sample time** – The data are sampled at points corresponding to multiples of the sample time. Therefore, the time span of the buffer corresponds to the length of the buffer times the sample time.

When you start the simulation, the Power Spectral Density block displays two plots:

- The time trajectory of the buffer

- The power spectral density with frequency on the x-axis

Click on the **DEMO** button in the Analyzer block library and then start the simulation to see the power spectral densities of various signals from the signal generator. The buffer is detrended to remove DC values, and a Hanning window is used to remove transient effects caused by the finite-length buffer. Overlapping and averaging are used if the number of points in the buffer is greater than the number of frequency points.

Average PSD (Power Spectral Density)

The Average PSD block is the same as the Power Spectral Density block, except that the frequency spectrum is averaged over time. It should be used in place of the Power Spectral Density block if you need a more accurate frequency spectrum of a signal.

This block uses the M-file sfunpsd.m.

Spectrum Analyzer

The Spectrum Analyzer block can be used to find the transfer function of a system in terms of a frequency plot by dividing the input and output FFTs of a system.

Drive the first input of the block with the input to your system (its forcing function) and the second input of the block with the output of the system. A graph of the estimated frequency response is returned. A more accurate representation of the block's frequency response can be found when you use input signals with a high harmonic content, such as noise.

The demo provided in the Analyzer block library requires the Signals and Systems Toolbox. It finds the frequency response of a discrete-time Chebychev band pass filter. The dialog entries of this block are the same as those of the Power Spectral Density block.

Averaging Spectrum Analyzer

The Averaging Spectrum Analyzer block is similar to the Spectrum Analyzer block, except that the frequency plot is averaged over time. This block should be used in place of the Spectrum Analyzer if you need to get a more accurate transfer function of a system.

Filters

Filter blocks contain a collection of digital (discrete-time) and analog (continuous-time) filters. They use filter design functions in the Signals and Systems Toolbox.

These blocks are designed using the masking feature, described in Chapter 5. The block icons display a frequency response based on the current values of their coefficients. The analog filter frequency plots are displayed on a log-log scale, whereas the discrete filters are displayed on a standard linear plot. The icons for some blocks may take some time to be displayed, since they must be recalculated every time a coefficient is changed and when they are opened for the first time.

The analog filters typically have parameters for cutoff frequency, order of the filter, and, possibly, bandwidth for bandpass and bandstop filters. Some filters require a parameter for the permissible ripple in the pass and/or stop bands.

The discrete filters contain a parameter for sample time. In most circumstances, the digital filters place less demand on the integration routines and, therefore, simulate faster. In certain cases, some integrators (e.g., euler, rk23, rk45, and adams) are not able to handle filters that have widely varying dynamics. Since the filters are linear, linsim generally produces fast and accurate simulations. You may want to reduce the maximum step-size so that linsim gives results at reasonably spaced intervals.

You can learn more about these blocks by unmasking them and looking at the appropriate toolbox function they call. For numerical accuracy, these blocks are implemented using State-Space and Zero-Pole blocks. For order less than eight, they are implemented in controller canonical form for faster calculation.

Index